The UK Tower Air Fryer Cookbook For Beginners

365 Days Easy and Affordable Recipes for the Whole Year incl.
Side Dishes, Desserts, Snacks and More

Edward J. Milton

Contents

Chapter 5 Fish and Seafood   26

Chapter 6 Beef, Pork, and Lamb   34

Chapter 7 Snacks and Appetisers   41

Chapter 8 Desserts   48

INTRODUCTION

The dynamics of cooking have taken a different turn in these days. Cooking has become enjoyable in the current days of advanced technology, and it's a progress that I admire ultimately. I would commend the efforts of all that have deemed it fit to ensure that kitchen equipment is available in different sizes and functions.

Of all the many cooking equipment we have today, the Tower Air Fryer is one of the best you can ever have. Apart from its considerable sizes, I can attest to the different functionalities of Tower Air Fryer. Therefore, the Tower Air Fryer is quite underrated, considering other options such as slow cooker, deep fryer, toaster oven, and good baking ovens.

In my experience of doing due diligence on new equipment, recipes are very important. Tower Air fryer should be considered, to a large extent, due to its recipes. You can begin to ask why, and that is because of its compatibility with different recipes.

I jokingly refer to tower air fryers as mini convection ovens, although they work in a time lesser than the convectional ovens will take. You can have different recipes of French fries, chicken wings, veggies cooked into a crispy meal in a tower air fryer. It is a process that I have gone through repeatedly and with a good success rate.

A healthy diet is important to me, so I always do the due diligence to find kitchen equipment that suits my needs at every instant. With my personal knowledge and experience of cooking with the tower air fryer, I have taken it upon myself to curate a cookbook that allows you to learn, practice and master the art of cooking with an air fryer.

I understand that cooking should be enjoyable, and as a result, this cookbook has been fortified with information across chapters to serve as a guide to help you achieve your perfect meal. I hope you have a nice read and memories to hold onto as you begin to read.

Happy reading!

Chapter 1 Tower Air Fryer Basic Guide

Chapter 1 Tower Air Fryer Basic Guide

In the simplest term, a Tower Air Fryer is a countertop oven. It is portable in size and works by allowing you to fry food without immersing it in hot oil. This process does not change the expected result or make your meal less delicious. This peculiar quality of not immersing food in hot oil makes it remarkable from other cooking appliances. In addition, the tower Air Fryer saves energy, allowing you to cook in 15 minutes and with different cooking options.

How does Tower Air Fryer work?

Let's delve into how the Tower Air Fryer works; it is a fascinating convection process. Start by cutting out the food you intend to fry. Then, place your food in the air fryer basket after you must have slid it out.

Foods are fried by hot air generated by a fan inside the Tower Air Fryer. The cooking process starts from the outside and goes inside to ensure that you cook the food in the air fryer basket.

With a Tower Air Fryer, you get an equal meal benefit as if you have used a slow cooker and a deep fryer. However, when cooking with a Tower Air Fryer, some grease might drop at the bottom of your air fryer. Don't worry; a small container is provided to catch it.

I encourage a gentle shaking of the Tower Air Fryer at intervals to ensure that all sizes of food in the basket are cooked evenly. From my experience, avoiding overloading the air fryer with food is smart. Whenever you need to use oil, try to use it a little and not be too generous with the oil.

Five Features of Tower Air Fryer

There are many features of the Tower Air Fryer, but we shall be looking at the crucial ones or those features that are most important. I see these five features as why the Tower Air Fryer stands out on the kitchen appliances list.

Less Fat

To maintain a healthy diet, I researched how the air fryer adds value in that regard. Tower Air Fryer requires little or no oil, which is a piece of good news and an improvement on other kitchen equipment that requires oil.

It is a good appliance for anyone with hypertension, hyperlipidemia, and other cardiovascular conditions. If your major concern is calories in food, it just got better as the air fryer ensures that only fat is lost and not flavor.

Faster meals

In this age, more people are busier than in the olden days. Therefore, it is logical that an average human would want to have food prepared in the shortest possible time.

I work on a tight schedule and cannot be grateful enough for how Tower Air Fryer saves time. Cooking food in 15 minutes is a great feature I think everyone should benefit from and utilize maximally.

Cooking just got easier, healthier, and faster!

More meal choices

To many, the Tower Air fryer seems to be an appliance that can only handle fries. However, the reality of this air fryer is its

usefulness in preparing many meal choices. Furthermore, the air fryer has different functions, such as fry, roast, grill, and bake. Therefore, you can conclude that not too much kitchen equipment has all the functions coupled with easy usage.

Less energy

For an average user of kitchen appliances or home appliances, considerable energy consumption is one feature to be treasured. From my own experience, most of the kitchen equipment is energy sapping. It will be wise to consider the ones that consume less energy.

With the energy-saving property, Tower Air Fryers use less power than conventional ovens. As a result, you can save up to 50 percent energy when cooking with the air fryer.

Enough capacity

Portability is an important feature of kitchen appliances. You don't want to struggle with your stuff while moving from one apartment to another.

Your air fryer can be portable yet with enough capacity to handle the size of your food. In addition, it is convenient to serve enough portions to members of your house due to the family-sized Tower Air Fryers.

A 4.5L capacity is certainly considerable!

Tower Air Fryer Cooking Tips

Like every other kitchen or home appliance, you must take time to read the appliance's dos and don'ts. Then, you get to see buttons that you can press to execute various cooking processes, compartments, etc.

Let us delve into the handling of the Tower Air Fryers. From the preparation for the use of the air fryer to the settings, we shall go through this journey in a stepwise manner.

Preparation for use

Like every other portable appliance, I recommend placing your air fryers on a horizontal and stable platform. In addition, you should place it on a heat-resistant surface because of emissions from the air fryer.

The air fryer comes with a basket; always remember to place it inside the drawer when you are ready to use it. Filling the drawer with oil or any liquid is not a good idea. Refrain from it!

Do not put anything on the appliance when using the air fryer, as that might hinder the hot air frying process. Remember that the appliance works by convection. As a result, airflow is crucial.

Air frying

It would be best if you had a preparation time for your food. It is the time it will take for all the ingredients to be cooked properly. There is always an in-built timer that comes with Tower Air Fryers. The air fryer stops when it has reached the zero mark, or you manually tweak it to the zero mark.

For air frying, you should connect the main plug to the earthed socket in your kitchen and pull out the drawer in a careful manner. You must have cut out your ingredients and put them into the air fryer basket.

Make a gentle sliding of the drawer back into the air fryer, and ensure you always use the drawer with the basket. Set the timer, and expect the hot air frying process to start by bringing out the working light. The light will come and go to indicate that it's working and maintain the temperature.

Avoid touching the drawer immediately after the timer stops, allow the surface to be cool, and you can handle it with a napkin. Of course, you can always check the ingredients after the timer stops and shake to restart the process.

Settings

I will always recommend that you have the right idea of what you are trying to make. In addition, the preparation time depends on your ingredients, which will also influence your decision regarding the settings.

As I said, there is no single manner to adjust your settings. It depends on the ingredients' origin, size, shape, and brands.

Generally, the air fryer should need a shorter cooking time for smaller ingredients and a considerable cooking time for larger ingredients.

Care and cleaning

Following these tips makes it very easy to keep your Tower Air Fryers clean and functional.

The drawer: ensure that you don't immerse the drawer inside water or any liquid. You can clean with some washing-up liquid and a non-abrasive sponge. Again, do not immerse inside any liquid!

The air fryer basket: should also be washed with a liquid and a non-abrasive sponge; remove it to allow it to cool down and wash up. You can make use of a degreasing liquid to remove sticky dirt.

The outside of the air fryer: it should be cleaned with a moist cloth after you must have removed the plug and allowed it to cool.

The inside of the air fryer: you can clean the inside with hot water and a non-abrasive sponge.

Ensure that the air fryer is cool before you wash it, then dry it, and you can progress to storing it in a cool and dry place.

Chapter 2 Breakfasts

Chapter 2 Breakfasts

Pita and Pepperoni Pizza

Prep time: 10 minutes | Cook time: 6 minutes | Serves 1

1 teaspoon olive oil
1 tablespoon ready-made pizza sauce
1 pita bread
6 pepperoni slices
30 g grated Mozzarella cheese
¼ teaspoon garlic powder
¼ teaspoon dried oregano

1. Preheat the air fryer to 176ºC. Grease the air fryer basket with olive oil. 2. Spread the pizza sauce on top of the pita bread. Put the pepperoni slices over the sauce, followed by the Mozzarella cheese. 3. Season with garlic powder and oregano. 4. Put the pita pizza inside the air fryer and place a trivet on top. 5. Bake in the preheated air fryer for 6 minutes and serve.

Breakfast Sammies

Prep time: 15 minutes | Cook time: 20 minutes | Serves 5

Biscuits:
6 large egg whites
250 g blanched almond flour, plus more if needed
1½ teaspoons baking powder
½ teaspoon fine sea salt
30 g very cold unsalted butter (or lard for dairy-free), cut into
¼-inch pieces
Eggs:
5 large eggs
½ teaspoon fine sea salt
¼ teaspoon ground black pepper
5 (30 g) slices Cheddar cheese (omit for dairy-free)
10 thin slices ham

1. Spray the air fryer basket with avocado oil. Preheat the air fryer to 176ºC. Grease two pie pans, or two baking pans that will fit inside your air fryer. 2. Make the biscuits: In a medium-sized bowl, whip the egg whites with a hand mixer until very stiff. Set aside. 3. In a separate medium-sized bowl, stir together the almond flour, baking powder, and salt until well combined. Cut in the butter. Gently fold the flour mixture into the egg whites with a rubber spatula. If the dough is too wet to form into mounds, add a few tablespoons of almond flour until the dough holds together well. 4. Using a large spoon, divide the dough into 5 equal portions and drop them about 1 inch apart on one of the greased pie pans. (If you're using a smaller air fryer, work in batches if necessary.) Place the pan in the air fryer and bake for 11 to 14 minutes, until the biscuits are golden brown. Remove from the air fryer and set aside to cool. 5. Make the eggs: Set the air fryer to 192ºC. Crack the eggs into the remaining greased pie pan and sprinkle with the salt and pepper. Place the eggs in the air fryer to bake for 5 minutes, or until they are cooked to your liking. 6. Open the air fryer and top each egg yolk with a slice of cheese (if using). Bake for another minute, or until the cheese is melted. 7. Once the biscuits are cool, slice them in half lengthwise. Place 1 cooked egg topped with cheese and 2 slices of ham in each biscuit. 8. Store leftover biscuits, eggs, and ham in separate airtight containers in the fridge for up to 3 days. Reheat the biscuits and eggs on a baking sheet in a preheated 176ºC air fryer for 5 minutes, or until warmed through.

Bacon, Broccoli and Cheese Bread Pudding

Prep time: 30 minutes | Cook time: 48 minutes | Serves 2 to 4

230 g thick cut bacon, cut into ¼-inch pieces
375 g brioche bread or rolls, cut into ½-inch cubes
3 eggs
250 ml milk
½ teaspoon salt
Freshly ground black pepper
125 g frozen broccoli florets, thawed and chopped
185 g grated Swiss cheese

1. Preheat the air fryer to 204ºC. 2. Air fry the bacon for 6 to 10 minutes until crispy, shaking the basket a few times while it cooks to help it cook evenly. Remove the bacon and set it aside on a paper towel. 3. Air fry the brioche bread cubes for 2 minutes to dry and toast lightly. (If your brioche is a few days old and slightly stale, you can omit this step.) 4. Butter a cake pan. Combine all the ingredients in a large bowl and toss well. Transfer the mixture to the buttered cake pan, cover with aluminum foil and refrigerate the bread pudding overnight, or for at least 8 hours. 5. Remove the casserole from the refrigerator an hour before you plan to cook, and let it sit on the countertop to come to room temperature. 6. Preheat the air fryer to 164ºC. Transfer the covered cake pan, to the basket of the air fryer, lowering the dish into the basket using a sling made of aluminum foil (fold a piece of aluminum foil into a strip about 2-inches wide by 24-inches long). Fold the ends of the aluminum foil over the top of the dish before returning the basket to the air fryer. Air fry for 20 minutes. Remove the foil and air fry for an additional 20 minutes. If the top starts to brown a little too much before the custard has set, simply return the foil to the pan. The bread pudding has cooked through when a skewer inserted into the center comes out clean.

Chimichanga Breakfast Burrito

Prep time: 10 minutes | Cook time: 10 minutes | Serves 2

2 large (10- to 12-inch) flour tortillas
60 g can refried beans (pinto or black beans work equally well)
4 large eggs, cooked scrambled
4 corn tortilla chips, crushed
60 g grated chilli Cheddar cheese
12 pickled jalapeño slices
1 tablespoon vegetable oil
Guacamole, salsa, and sour cream, for serving (optional)

1. Place the tortillas on a work surface and divide the refried beans between them, spreading them in a rough rectangle in the center of the tortillas. Top the beans with the scrambled eggs, crushed chips, cheese, and jalapeños. Fold one side over the fillings, then fold in each short side and roll up the rest of the way like a burrito. 2. Brush the outside of the burritos with the oil, then transfer to the air fryer, seam-side down. Air fry at 176ºC until the tortillas are browned and crisp and the filling is warm throughout, about 10 minutes. 3. Transfer the chimichangas to plates and serve warm with guacamole, salsa, and sour cream, if you like.

Simple Cinnamon Toasts

Prep time: 5 minutes | Cook time: 4 minutes | Serves 4

1 tablespoon salted butter
2 teaspoons ground cinnamon
4 tablespoons sugar
½ teaspoon vanilla extract
10 bread slices

1. Preheat the air fryer to 192°C. 2. In a bowl, combine the butter, cinnamon, sugar, and vanilla extract. Spread onto the slices of bread. 3. Put the bread inside the air fryer and bake for 4 minutes or until golden brown. 4. Serve warm.

Western Frittata

Prep time: 10 minutes | Cook time: 19 minutes | Serves 1 to 2

½ red or green bell pepper, cut into ½-inch chunks
1 teaspoon olive oil
3 eggs, beaten
30 g grated Cheddar cheese
30 g diced cooked ham
Salt and freshly ground black pepper, to taste
1 teaspoon butter
1 teaspoon chopped fresh parsley

1. Preheat the air fryer to 204°C. 2. Toss the peppers with the olive oil and air fry for 6 minutes, shaking the basket once or twice during the cooking process to redistribute the ingredients. 3. While the vegetables are cooking, beat the eggs well in a bowl, stir in the Cheddar cheese and ham, and season with salt and freshly ground black pepper. Add the air-fried peppers to this bowl when they have finished cooking. 4. Place a cake pan into the air fryer basket with the butter, using an aluminum sling to lower the pan into the basket. Air fry for 1 minute at 192°C to melt the butter. Remove the cake pan and rotate the pan to distribute the butter and grease the pan. Pour the egg mixture into the cake pan and return the pan to the air fryer, using the aluminum sling. 5. Air fry at 192°C for 12 minutes, or until the frittata has puffed up and is lightly browned. Let the frittata sit in the air fryer for 5 minutes to cool to an edible temperature and set up. Remove the cake pan from the air fryer, sprinkle with parsley and serve immediately.

Parmesan Sausage Egg Muffins

Prep time: 5 minutes | Cook time: 20 minutes | Serves 4

170 g Italian-recipe sausage, sliced
6 eggs
30 g heavy cream
Salt and ground black pepper, to taste
85 g Parmesan cheese, grated

1. Preheat the air fryer to 176°C. Grease a muffin pan. 2. Put the sliced sausage in the muffin pan. 3. Beat the eggs with the cream in a bowl and season with salt and pepper. 4. Pour half of the mixture over the sausages in the pan. 5. Sprinkle with cheese and the remaining egg mixture. 6. Bake in the preheated air fryer for 20 minutes or until set. 7. Serve immediately.

Pizza Eggs

Prep time: 5 minutes | Cook time: 10 minutes | Serves 2

125 g shredded Mozzarella cheese
7 slices pepperoni, chopped
1 large egg, whisked
¼ teaspoon dried oregano
¼ teaspoon dried parsley
¼ teaspoon garlic powder
¼ teaspoon salt

1. Place Mozzarella in a single layer on the bottom of an ungreased round nonstick baking dish. Scatter pepperoni over the cheese, then pour egg evenly around baking dish. 2. Sprinkle with remaining ingredients and place into air fryer basket. Adjust the temperature to 164°C and bake for 10 minutes. When cheese is brown and egg is set, dish will be done. 3. Let cool in dish 5 minutes before serving.

Cinnamon Rolls

Prep time: 10 minutes | Cook time: 20 minutes | Makes 12 rolls

310 g shredded Mozzarella cheese
60 g cream cheese, softened
125 g blanched finely ground
almond flour
½ teaspoon vanilla extract
60 g powdered sweetener
1 tablespoon ground cinnamon

1. In a large microwave-safe bowl, combine Mozzarella cheese, cream cheese, and flour. Microwave the mixture on high 90 seconds until cheese is melted. 2. Add vanilla extract and sweetener, and mix 2 minutes until a dough forms. 3. Once the dough is cool enough to work with your hands, about 2 minutes, spread it out into a 12 × 4 inch rectangle on ungreased baking paper. Evenly sprinkle dough with cinnamon. 4. Starting at the long side of the dough, roll lengthwise to form a log. Slice the log into twelve even pieces. 5. Divide rolls between two ungreased, round nonstick baking dishes. Place one dish into air fryer basket. Adjust the temperature to 192°C and bake for 10 minutes. 6. Cinnamon rolls will be done when golden around the edges and mostly firm. Repeat with second dish. Allow rolls to cool in dishes 10 minutes before serving.

Bacon, Cheese, and Avocado Melt

Prep time: 5 minutes | Cook time: 3 to 5 minutes | Serves 2

1 avocado
4 slices cooked bacon, chopped
2 tablespoons salsa
1 tablespoon heavy cream
30 g shredded Cheddar cheese

1. Preheat the air fryer to 204°C. 2. Slice the avocado in half lengthwise and remove the stone. To ensure the avocado halves do not roll in the basket, slice a thin piece of skin off the base. 3. In a small bowl, combine the bacon, salsa, and cream. Divide the mixture between the avocado halves and top with the cheese. 4. Place the avocado halves in the air fryer basket and air fry for 3 to 5 minutes until the cheese has melted and begins to brown. Serve warm.

Cheesy Bell Pepper Eggs

Prep time: 10 minutes | Cook time: 15 minutes | Serves 4

4 medium green bell peppers
85 g cooked ham, chopped
¼ medium onion, peeled and

chopped
8 large eggs
125 g mild Cheddar cheese

1. Cut the tops off each bell pepper. Remove the seeds and the white membranes with a small knife. Place ham and onion into each pepper. 2. Crack 2 eggs into each pepper. Top with 30 g cheese per pepper. Place into the air fryer basket. 3. Adjust the temperature to 200°C and air fry for 15 minutes. 4. When fully cooked, peppers will be tender and eggs will be firm. Serve immediately.

Breakfast Pizza

Prep time: 5 minutes | Cook time: 8 minutes | Serves 1

2 large eggs
60 ml unsweetened, unflavored almond milk (or unflavored hemp milk for nut-free)
¼ teaspoon fine sea salt
⅛ teaspoon ground black pepper
30 g diced onions

30 g shredded Parmesan cheese (omit for dairy-free)
6 pepperoni slices (omit for vegetarian)
¼ teaspoon dried oregano leaves
60 g pizza sauce, warmed, for serving

1. Preheat the air fryer to 176°C. Grease a cake pan. 2. In a small bowl, use a fork to whisk together the eggs, almond milk, salt, and pepper. Add the onions and stir to mix. Pour the mixture into the greased pan. Top with the cheese (if using), pepperoni slices (if using), and oregano. 3. Place the pan in the air fryer and bake for 8 minutes, or until the eggs are cooked to your liking. 4. Loosen the eggs from the sides of the pan with a spatula and place them on a serving plate. Drizzle the pizza sauce on top. Best served fresh.

Nutty Granola

Prep time: 5 minutes | Cook time: 1 hour | Serves 4

60 g pecans, coarsely chopped
60 g walnuts or almonds, coarsely chopped
30 g unsweetened desiccated coconut
30 g almond flour
30 g ground flaxseed or chia seeds

2 tablespoons sunflower seeds
2 tablespoons melted butter
30 g granulated sweetener
½ teaspoon ground cinnamon
½ teaspoon vanilla extract
¼ teaspoon ground nutmeg
¼ teaspoon salt
2 tablespoons water

1. Preheat the air fryer to 120°C. Cut a piece of baking paper to fit inside the air fryer basket. 2. In a large bowl, toss the nuts, coconut, almond flour, ground flaxseed or chia seeds, sunflower seeds, butter, sweetener, cinnamon, vanilla, nutmeg, salt, and water until thoroughly combined. 3. Spread the granola on the baking paper and flatten to an even thickness. 4. Air fry for about an hour, or until golden throughout. Remove from the air fryer and allow to fully cool. Break the granola into bite-sized pieces and store in a covered container for up to a week.

Cauliflower Avocado Toast

Prep time: 15 minutes | Cook time: 8 minutes | Serves 2

1 (340 g) steam bag cauliflower
1 large egg
60 g shredded Mozzarella cheese

1 ripe medium avocado
½ teaspoon garlic powder
¼ teaspoon ground black pepper

1. Cook cauliflower according to package instructions. Remove from bag and place into cheesecloth or clean towel to remove excess moisture. 2. Place cauliflower into a large bowl and mix in egg and Mozzarella. Cut a piece of baking paper to fit your air fryer basket. Separate the cauliflower mixture into two, and place it on the baking paper in two mounds. Press out the cauliflower mounds into a ¼-inch-thick rectangle. Place the baking paper into the air fryer basket. 3. Adjust the temperature to 204°C and set the timer for 8 minutes. 4. Flip the cauliflower halfway through the cooking time. 5. When the timer beeps, remove the baking paper and allow the cauliflower to cool 5 minutes. 6. Cut open the avocado and remove the pit. Scoop out the inside, place it in a medium bowl, and mash it with garlic powder and pepper. Spread onto the cauliflower. Serve immediately.

Cheddar-Ham-Corn Muffins

Prep time: 10 minutes | Cook time: 6 to 8 minutes per batch | Makes 8 muffins

95 g yellow cornmeal
30 g flour
1½ teaspoons baking powder
¼ teaspoon salt
1 egg, beaten
2 tablespoons rapeseed oil
125 ml milk

60 g shredded sharp Cheddar cheese
60 g diced ham
8 foil muffin cups, liners removed and sprayed with cooking spray

1. Preheat the air fryer to 200°C. 2. In a medium bowl, stir together the cornmeal, flour, baking powder, and salt. 3. Add egg, oil, and milk to dry ingredients and mix well. 4. Stir in shredded cheese and diced ham. 5. Divide batter among the muffin cups. 6. Place 4 filled muffin cups in air fryer basket and bake for 5 minutes. 7. Reduce temperature to 164°C and bake for 1 to 2 minutes or until toothpick inserted in center of muffin comes out clean. 8. Repeat steps 6 and 7 to cook remaining muffins.

Gold Avocado

Prep time: 5 minutes | Cook time: 6 minutes | Serves 4

2 large avocados, sliced
¼ teaspoon paprika
Salt and ground black pepper, to taste

60 g plain flour
2 eggs, beaten
125 g bread crumbs

1. Preheat the air fryer to 204°C. 2. Sprinkle paprika, salt and pepper on the slices of avocado. 3. Lightly coat the avocados with flour. Dredge them in the eggs, before covering with bread crumbs. 4. Transfer to the air fryer and air fry for 6 minutes. 5. Serve warm.

Parmesan Ranch Risotto

Prep time: 10 minutes | Cook time: 30 minutes | Serves 2

1 tablespoon olive oil	95 g Arborio rice
1 clove garlic, minced	500 ml chicken stock, boiling
1 tablespoon unsalted butter	60 g Parmesan cheese, grated
1 onion, diced	

1. Preheat the air fryer to 200ºC. 2. Grease a round baking tin with olive oil and stir in the garlic, butter, and onion. 3. Transfer the tin to the air fryer and bake for 4 minutes. Add the rice and bake for 4 more minutes. 4. Turn the air fryer to 160ºC and pour in the chicken stock. Cover and bake for 22 minutes. 5. Scatter with cheese and serve.

Cheesy Cauliflower "Hash Browns"

Prep time: 30 minutes | Cook time: 24 minutes | Makes 6 hash browns

60 g 100% cheese crisps	1 large egg
1 (340 g) steam bag cauliflower, cooked according to package instructions	60 g shredded sharp Cheddar cheese
	½ teaspoon salt

1. Let cooked cauliflower cool 10 minutes. 2. Place cheese crisps into food processor and pulse on low 30 seconds until crisps are finely ground. 3. Using a kitchen towel, wring out excess moisture from cauliflower and place into food processor. 4. Add egg to food processor and sprinkle with Cheddar and salt. Pulse five times until mixture is mostly smooth. 5. Cut two pieces of baking paper to fit air fryer basket. Separate mixture into six even scoops and place three on each piece of ungreased baking paper, keeping at least 2 inch of space between each scoop. Press each into a hash brown shape, about ¼ inch thick. 6. Place one batch on baking paper into air fryer basket. Adjust the temperature to 192ºC and air fry for 12 minutes, turning hash browns halfway through cooking. Hash browns will be golden brown when done. Repeat with second batch. 7. Allow 5 minutes to cool. Serve warm.

Johnny Cakes

Prep time: 10 minutes | Cook time: 10 to 12 minutes | Serves 4

60 g plain flour	250 ml milk, whole or semi-skimmed
185 g yellow cornmeal	
2 tablespoons sugar	1 tablespoon butter, melted
1 teaspoon baking powder	1 large egg, lightly beaten
1 teaspoon salt	1 to 2 tablespoons oil

1. In a large bowl, whisk the flour, cornmeal, sugar, baking powder, and salt until blended. Whisk in the milk, melted butter, and egg until the mixture is sticky but still lumpy. 2. Preheat the air fryer to 176ºC. Line the air fryer basket with baking paper. 3. For each cake, drop 1 heaping tablespoon of batter onto the baking paper. The fryer should hold 4 cakes. 4. Spritz the cakes with oil and cook for 3 minutes. Turn the cakes, spritz with oil again, and cook for 2 to 3 minutes more. Repeat with a second batch of cakes.

Turkey Breakfast Sausage Patties

Prep time: 5 minutes | Cook time: 10 minutes | Serves 4

1 tablespoon chopped fresh thyme	½ teaspoon garlic powder
1 tablespoon chopped fresh sage	⅛ teaspoon crushed red pepper flakes
1¼ teaspoons kosher or coarse sea salt	⅛ teaspoon freshly ground black pepper
1 teaspoon chopped fennel seeds	450 g 93% lean minced turkey
¾ teaspoon smoked paprika	60 g finely minced sweet apple (peeled)
½ teaspoon onion powder	

1. Thoroughly combine the thyme, sage, salt, fennel seeds, paprika, onion powder, garlic powder, red pepper flakes, and black pepper in a medium bowl. 2. Add the ground turkey and apple and stir until well incorporated. Divide the mixture into 8 equal portions and shape into patties with your hands, each about ¼ inch thick and 3 inches in diameter. 3. Preheat the air fryer to 204ºC. 4. Place the patties in the air fryer basket in a single layer. You may need to work in batches to avoid overcrowding. 5. Air fry for 5 minutes. Flip the patties and air fry for 5 minutes, or until the patties are nicely browned and cooked through. 6. Remove from the basket to a plate and repeat with the remaining patties. 7. Serve warm.

Simple Scotch Eggs

Prep time: 5 minutes | Cook time: 25 minutes | Serves 4

4 large hard boiled eggs	8 slices thick-cut bacon
1 (340 g) package pork sausage-meat	4 wooden toothpicks, soaked in water for at least 30 minutes

1. Slice the sausage into four parts and place each part into a large circle. 2. Put an egg into each circle and wrap it in the sausage. Put in the refrigerator for 1 hour. 3. Preheat the air fryer to 232ºC. 4. Make a cross with two pieces of thick-cut bacon. Put a wrapped egg in the center, fold the bacon over top of the egg, and secure with a toothpick. 5. Air fry in the preheated air fryer for 25 minutes. 6. Serve immediately.

Spinach Omelet

Prep time: 5 minutes | Cook time: 12 minutes | Serves 2

4 large eggs	2 tablespoons salted butter, melted
30 g chopped fresh spinach leaves	
2 tablespoons peeled and chopped yellow onion	60 g shredded mild Cheddar cheese
	¼ teaspoon salt

1. In an ungreased round nonstick baking dish, whisk eggs. Stir in spinach, onion, butter, Cheddar, and salt. 2. Place dish into air fryer basket. Adjust the temperature to 160ºC and bake for 12 minutes. Omelet will be done when browned on the top and firm in the middle. 3. Slice in half and serve warm on two medium plates.

Veggie Frittata

Prep time: 7 minutes | Cook time: 21 to 23 minutes | Serves 2

Avocado oil spray
30 g diced red onion
30 g diced red bell pepper
30 g finely chopped broccoli

4 large eggs
85 g shredded sharp Cheddar cheese, divided
½ teaspoon dried thyme
Sea salt and freshly ground black pepper, to taste

1. Spray a pan well with oil. Put the onion, pepper, and broccoli in the pan, place the pan in the air fryer, and set to 176ºC. Bake for 5 minutes. 2. While the vegetables cook, beat the eggs in a medium bowl. Stir in half of the cheese, and season with the thyme, salt, and pepper. 3. Add the eggs to the pan and top with the remaining cheese. Set the air fryer to 176ºC. Bake for 16 to 18 minutes, until cooked through.

Breakfast Pita

Prep time: 5 minutes | Cook time: 6 minutes | Serves 2

1 whole wheat pita
2 teaspoons olive oil
½ shallot, diced
¼ teaspoon garlic, minced
1 large egg

¼ teaspoon dried oregano
¼ teaspoon dried thyme
⅛ teaspoon salt
2 tablespoons shredded Parmesan cheese

1. Preheat the air fryer to 192ºC. 2. Brush the top of the pita with olive oil, then spread the diced shallot and minced garlic over the pita. 3. Crack the egg into a small bowl or ramekin, and season it with oregano, thyme, and salt. 4. Place the pita into the air fryer basket, and gently pour the egg onto the top of the pita. Sprinkle with cheese over the top. 5. Bake for 6 minutes. 6. Allow to cool for 5 minutes before cutting into pieces for serving.

Baked Peach Oatmeal

Prep time: 5 minutes | Cook time: 30 minutes | Serves 6

Olive oil cooking spray
250 g certified gluten-free rolled oats
500 ml unsweetened almond milk
60 g raw honey, plus more for drizzling (optional)
125 g nonfat plain Greek yogurt

1 teaspoon vanilla extract
½ teaspoon ground cinnamon
¼ teaspoon salt
185 g diced peaches, divided, plus more for serving (optional)

1. Preheat the air fryer to 192ºC. Lightly coat the inside of a 6-inch cake pan with olive oil cooking spray. 2. In a large bowl, mix together the oats, almond milk, honey, yogurt, vanilla, cinnamon, and salt until well combined. 3. Fold in 95 g peaches and then pour the mixture into the prepared cake pan. 4. Sprinkle the remaining peaches across the top of the oatmeal mixture. Bake in the air fryer for 30 minutes. 5. Allow to set and cool for 5 minutes before serving with additional fresh fruit and honey for drizzling, if desired.

Chapter 3 Vegetables and Sides

Chapter 3 Vegetables and Sides

"Faux-Tato" Hash

Prep time: 10 minutes | Cook time: 12 minutes | Serves 4

450 g radishes, ends removed, quartered
¼ medium yellow onion, peeled and diced
½ medium green bell pepper,
seeded and chopped
2 tablespoons salted butter, melted
½ teaspoon garlic powder
¼ teaspoon ground black pepper

1. In a large bowl, combine radishes, onion, and bell pepper. Toss with butter. 2. Sprinkle garlic powder and black pepper over mixture in bowl, then spoon into ungreased air fryer basket. 3. Adjust the temperature to 160°C and air fry for 12 minutes. Shake basket halfway through cooking. Radishes will be tender when done. Serve warm.

Corn Croquettes

Prep time: 10 minutes | Cook time: 12 to 14 minutes | Serves 4

60 g leftover mashed potatoes
250 g sweetcorn kernels (if frozen, thawed, and well drained)
¼ teaspoon onion powder
⅛ teaspoon ground black pepper
¼ teaspoon salt
60 g panko bread crumbs
Oil for misting or cooking spray

1. Place the potatoes and half the sweetcorn in food processor and pulse until well chopped. 2. Transfer mixture to large bowl and stir in remaining sweetcorn, onion powder, pepper and salt. 3. Shape mixture into 16 balls. 4. Roll balls in panko crumbs, mist with oil or cooking spray, and place in air fryer basket. 5. Air fry at 180°C for 12 to 14 minutes, until golden brown and crispy.

Ricotta Potatoes

Prep time: 15 minutes | Cook time: 15 minutes | Serves 4

4 potatoes
2 tablespoons olive oil
60 g Ricotta cheese, at room temperature
2 tablespoons chopped spring onions
1 tablespoon roughly chopped
fresh parsley
1 tablespoon minced coriander
60 g Cheddar cheese, preferably freshly grated
1 teaspoon celery seeds
½ teaspoon salt
½ teaspoon garlic pepper

1. Preheat the air fryer to 176°C. 2. Pierce the skin of the potatoes with a knife. 3. Air fry in the air fryer basket for 13 minutes. If they are not cooked through by this time, leave for 2 to 3 minutes longer. 4. In the meantime, make the stuffing by combining all the other ingredients. 5. Cut halfway into the cooked potatoes to open them. 6. Spoon equal amounts of the stuffing into each potato and serve hot.

Lemon garlic Mushrooms

Prep time: 10 minutes | Cook time: 10 to 15 minutes | Serves 6

340 g sliced mushrooms
1 tablespoon avocado oil
Sea salt and freshly ground black pepper, to taste
3 tablespoons unsalted butter
1 teaspoon minced garlic
1 teaspoon freshly squeezed lemon juice
½ teaspoon red pepper flakes
2 tablespoons chopped fresh parsley

1. Place the mushrooms in a medium bowl and toss with the oil. Season to taste with salt and pepper. 2. Place the mushrooms in a single layer in the air fryer basket. Set your air fryer to 192°C and roast for 10 to 15 minutes, until the mushrooms are tender. 3. While the mushrooms cook, melt the butter in a small pot or skillet over medium-low heat. Stir in the garlic and cook for 30 seconds. Remove the pot from the heat and stir in the lemon juice and red pepper flakes. 4. Toss the mushrooms with the lemon garlic butter and garnish with the parsley before serving.

Roasted Brussels Sprouts with Bacon

Prep time: 10 minutes | Cook time: 20 minutes | Serves 4

4 slices thick-cut bacon, chopped (about 115 g)
450 g Brussels sprouts, halved
(or quartered if large)
Freshly ground black pepper, to taste

1. Preheat the air fryer to 192°C. 2. Air fry the bacon for 5 minutes, shaking the basket once or twice during the cooking time. 3. Add the Brussels sprouts to the basket and drizzle a little bacon fat from the bottom of the air fryer drawer into the basket. Toss the sprouts to coat with the bacon fat. Air fry for an additional 15 minutes, or until the Brussels sprouts are tender to a knifepoint. 4. Season with freshly ground black pepper.

Rosemary New Potatoes

Prep time: 10 minutes | Cook time: 5 to 6 minutes | Serves 4

3 large red potatoes, sliced
¼ teaspoon ground rosemary
¼ teaspoon ground thyme
⅛ teaspoon salt
⅛ teaspoon ground black pepper
2 teaspoons extra-light olive oil

1. Preheat the air fryer to 164°C. 2. Place potatoes in large bowl and sprinkle with rosemary, thyme, salt, and pepper. 3. Stir with a spoon to distribute seasonings evenly. 4. Add oil to potatoes and stir again to coat well. 5. Air fry at 164°C for 4 minutes. Stir and break apart any that have stuck together. 6. Cook an additional 1 to 2 minutes or until fork-tender.

Dijon Roast Cabbage

Prep time: 10 minutes | Cook time: 10 minutes | Serves 4

1 small head cabbage, cored and sliced into 1-inch-thick slices
2 tablespoons olive oil, divided
½ teaspoon salt
1 tablespoon Dijon mustard
1 teaspoon apple cider vinegar
1 teaspoon granulated sweetener

1. Drizzle each cabbage slice with 1 tablespoon olive oil, then sprinkle with salt. Place slices into ungreased air fryer basket, working in batches if needed. Adjust the temperature to 176ºC and air fry for 10 minutes. Cabbage will be tender and edges will begin to brown when done. 2. In a small bowl, whisk remaining olive oil with mustard, vinegar, and sweetener. Drizzle over cabbage in a large serving dish. Serve warm.

Golden Pickles

Prep time: 10 minutes | Cook time: 15 minutes | Serves 4

14 dill pickles, sliced
30 g plain flour
⅛ teaspoon baking powder
Pinch of salt
2 tablespoons cornflour plus 3
tablespoons water
6 tablespoons panko bread crumbs
½ teaspoon paprika
Cooking spray

1. Preheat the air fryer to 204ºC. 2. Drain any excess moisture out of the dill pickles on a paper towel. 3. In a bowl, combine the flour, baking powder and salt. 4. Throw in the cornflour and water mixture and combine well with a whisk. 5. Put the panko bread crumbs in a shallow dish along with the paprika. Mix thoroughly. 6. Dip the pickles in the flour batter, before coating in the bread crumbs. Spritz all the pickles with the cooking spray. 7. Transfer to the air fryer basket and air fry for 15 minutes, or until golden brown. 8. Serve immediately.

Asparagus Fries

Prep time: 15 minutes | Cook time: 5 to 7 minutes per batch | Serves 4

340 g fresh asparagus spears with tough ends trimmed off
2 egg whites
60 ml water
95 g Panko bread crumbs
60 g grated Parmesan cheese, plus 2 tablespoons
¼ teaspoon salt
Oil for misting or cooking spray

1. Preheat the air fryer to 200ºC. 2. In a shallow dish, beat egg whites and water until slightly foamy. 3. In another shallow dish, combine panko, Parmesan, and salt. 4. Dip asparagus spears in egg, then roll in crumbs. Spray with oil or cooking spray. 5. Place a layer of asparagus in air fryer basket, leaving just a little space in between each spear. Stack another layer on top, crosswise. Air fry at 200ºC for 5 to 7 minutes, until crispy and golden brown. 6. Repeat to cook remaining asparagus.

Easy Greek Briami (Ratatouille)

Prep time: 15 minutes | Cook time: 40 minutes | Serves 6

2 russet potatoes, cubed
60 g plum tomatoes, cubed
1 aubergine, cubed
1 courgette, cubed
1 red onion, chopped
1 red bell pepper, chopped
2 garlic cloves, minced
1 teaspoon dried mint
1 teaspoon dried parsley
1 teaspoon dried oregano
½ teaspoon salt
½ teaspoon black pepper
¼ teaspoon red pepper flakes
85 ml olive oil
1 (230 g) can tomato paste
60 ml vegetable broth
60 ml water

1. Preheat the air fryer to 160ºC. 2. In a large bowl, combine the potatoes, tomatoes, aubergine, courgette, onion, bell pepper, garlic, mint, parsley, oregano, salt, black pepper, and red pepper flakes. 3. In a small bowl, mix together the olive oil, tomato paste, broth, and water. 4. Pour the oil-and-tomato-paste mixture over the vegetables and toss until everything is coated. 5. Pour the coated vegetables into the air fryer basket in an even layer and roast for 20 minutes. After 20 minutes, stir well and spread out again. Roast for an additional 10 minutes, then repeat the process and cook for another 10 minutes.

Indian Aubergine Bharta

Prep time: 15 minutes | Cook time: 20 minutes | Serves 4

1 medium aubergine
2 tablespoons vegetable oil
60 g finely minced onion
60 g finely chopped fresh tomato
2 tablespoons fresh lemon juice
2 tablespoons chopped fresh coriander
½ teaspoon kosher or coarse salt
⅛ teaspoon cayenne pepper

1. Rub the aubergine all over with the vegetable oil. Place the aubergine in the air fryer basket. Set the air fryer to 204ºC for 20 minutes, or until the aubergine skin is blistered and charred. 2. Transfer the aubergine to a large sandwich bag, seal, and set aside for 15 to 20 minutes (the aubergine will finish cooking in the residual heat trapped in the bag). 3. Transfer the aubergine to a large bowl. Peel off and discard the charred skin. Roughly mash the aubergine flesh. Add the onion, tomato, lemon juice, coriander, salt, and cayenne. Stir to combine.

Spiced Butternut Squash

Prep time: 10 minutes | Cook time: 15 minutes | Serves 4

500 g 1-inch-cubed butternut squash
2 tablespoons vegetable oil
1 to 2 tablespoons brown sugar
1 teaspoon Chinese five-spice powder

1. In a medium bowl, combine the squash, oil, sugar, and five-spice powder. Toss to coat. 2. Place the squash in the air fryer basket. Set the air fryer to 204ºC for 15 minutes or until tender.

Spinach and Sweet Pepper Poppers

Prep time: 10 minutes | Cook time: 8 minutes | Makes 16 poppers

115 g cream cheese, softened
20 g chopped fresh spinach leaves
½ teaspoon garlic powder

8 mini sweet bell peppers, tops removed, seeded, and halved lengthwise

1. In a medium bowl, mix cream cheese, spinach, and garlic powder. Place 1 tablespoon mixture into each sweet pepper half and press down to smooth. 2. Place poppers into ungreased air fryer basket. Adjust the temperature to 204ºC and air fry for 8 minutes. Poppers will be done when cheese is browned on top and peppers are tender-crisp. Serve warm.

Gold Artichoke Hearts

Prep time: 15 minutes | Cook time: 8 minutes | Serves 4

12 whole artichoke hearts packed in water, drained
60 g plain flour
1 egg

40 g panko bread crumbs
1 teaspoon Italian seasoning
Cooking oil spray

1. Squeeze any excess water from the artichoke hearts and place them on paper towels to dry. 2. Place the flour in a small bowl. 3. In another small bowl, beat the egg. 4. In a third small bowl, stir together the panko and Italian seasoning. 5. Dip the artichoke hearts in the flour, in the egg, and into the panko mixture until coated. 6. Insert the crisper plate into the basket and the basket into the unit. Preheat the unit by selecting AIR FRY, setting the temperature to 192ºC, and setting the time to 3 minutes. Select START/STOP to begin. 7. Once the unit is preheated, spray the crisper plate and the basket with cooking oil. Place the breaded artichoke hearts into the basket, stacking them if needed. 8. Select AIR FRY, set the temperature to 192ºC, and set the time to 8 minutes. Select START/STOP to begin. 9. After 4 minutes, use tongs to flip the artichoke hearts. I recommend flipping instead of shaking because the hearts are small, and this will help keep the breading intact. Re-insert the basket to resume cooking. 10. When the cooking is complete, the artichoke hearts should be deep golden brown and crisp. Cool for 5 minutes before serving.

Shishito Pepper Roast

Prep time: 4 minutes | Cook time: 9 minutes | Serves 4

Cooking oil spray (sunflower, safflower, or refined coconut)
450 g Shishito, Anaheim, or bell peppers, rinsed

1 tablespoon soy sauce
2 teaspoons freshly squeezed lime juice
2 large garlic cloves, pressed

1. Insert the crisper plate into the basket and the basket into the unit. Preheat the unit by selecting AIR ROAST, setting the temperature to 200ºC, and setting the time to 3 minutes. Select START/STOP to begin. 2. Once the unit is preheated, spray the crisper plate and the basket with cooking oil. Place the peppers into the basket and spray them with oil. 3. Select AIR ROAST, set the temperature to 200ºC, and set the time to 9 minutes. Select START/STOP to begin. 4. After 3 minutes, remove the basket and shake the peppers. Spray the peppers with more oil. Reinsert the basket to resume cooking. Repeat this step again after 3 minutes. 5. While the peppers roast, in a medium bowl, whisk the soy sauce, lime juice, and garlic until combined. Set aside. 6. When the cooking is complete, several of the peppers should have lots of nice browned spots on them. If using Anaheim or bell peppers, cut a slit in the side of each pepper and remove the seeds, which can be bitter. 7. Place the roasted peppers in the bowl with the sauce. Toss to coat the peppers evenly and serve.

Green Tomato Salad

Prep time: 10 minutes | Cook time: 8 to 10 minutes | Serves 4

4 green tomatoes
½ teaspoon salt
1 large egg, lightly beaten
60 g peanut flour
1 tablespoon Creole seasoning
1 (140 g) bag rocket
Buttermilk Dressing:
250 g mayonnaise
125 g sour cream

2 teaspoons fresh lemon juice
2 tablespoons finely chopped fresh parsley
1 teaspoon dried dill
1 teaspoon dried chives
½ teaspoon salt
½ teaspoon garlic powder
½ teaspoon onion powder

1. Preheat the air fryer to 204ºC. 2. Slice the tomatoes into ½-inch slices and sprinkle with the salt. Let sit for 5 to 10 minutes. 3. Place the egg in a small shallow bowl. In another small shallow bowl, combine the peanut flour and Creole seasoning. Dip each tomato slice into the egg wash, then dip into the peanut flour mixture, turning to coat evenly. 4. Working in batches if necessary, arrange the tomato slices in a single layer in the air fryer basket and spray both sides lightly with olive oil. Air fry until browned and crisp, 8 to 10 minutes. 5. To make the buttermilk dressing: In a small bowl, whisk together the mayonnaise, sour cream, lemon juice, parsley, dill, chives, salt, garlic powder, and onion powder. 6. Serve the tomato slices on top of a bed of the arugula with the dressing on the side.

Mexican Corn in a Cup

Prep time: 5 minutes | Cook time: 10 minutes | Serves 4

500 g frozen sweetcorn kernels (do not thaw)
Vegetable oil spray
2 tablespoons butter
60 g sour cream
60 g mayonnaise
30 g grated Parmesan cheese (or feta, cotija, or queso fresco)

2 tablespoons fresh lemon or lime juice
1 teaspoon chilli powder
Chopped fresh green onion (optional)
Chopped fresh coriander (optional)

1. Place the sweetcorn in the bottom of the air fryer basket and spray with vegetable oil spray. Set the air fryer to 176ºC for 10 minutes. 2. Transfer the sweetcorn to a serving bowl. Add the butter and stir until melted. Add the sour cream, mayonnaise, cheese, lemon juice, and chilli powder; stir until well combined. Serve immediately with green onion and coriander (if using).

Kohlrabi Fries

Prep time: 10 minutes | Cook time: 20 to 30 minutes | Serves 4

910 g kohlrabi, peeled and cut into ¼ to ½-inch fries
2 tablespoons olive oil

Salt and freshly ground black pepper, to taste

1. Preheat the air fryer to 204ºC. 2. In a large bowl, combine the kohlrabi and olive oil. Season to taste with salt and black pepper. Toss gently until thoroughly coated. 3. Working in batches if necessary, spread the kohlrabi in a single layer in the air fryer basket. Pausing halfway through the cooking time to shake the basket, air fry for 20 to 30 minutes until the fries are lightly browned and crunchy.

Curried Fruit

Prep time: 10 minutes | Cook time: 20 minutes | Serves 6 to 8

125 g cubed fresh pineapple
125 g cubed fresh pear (firm, not overly ripe)
230 g frozen peaches, thawed

1 (425 g) can dark, sweet, pitted cherries with juice
2 tablespoons brown sugar
1 teaspoon curry powder

1. Combine all ingredients in large bowl. Stir gently to mix in the sugar and curry. 2. Pour into a baking pan and bake at 184ºC for 10 minutes. 3. Stir fruit and cook 10 more minutes. 4. Serve hot.
Hasselback Potatoes with Chive Pesto
Prep time: 10 minutes | Cook time: 40 minutes | Serves 2
2 medium russet potatoes

5 tablespoons olive oil

Kosher or coarse sea salt and freshly ground black pepper, to taste

5 g roughly chopped fresh chives
2 tablespoons packed fresh flat-leaf parsley leaves
1 tablespoon chopped walnuts

1 tablespoon grated Parmesan cheese
1 teaspoon fresh lemon juice
1 small garlic clove, peeled
60 g sour cream

1. Place the potatoes on a cutting board and lay a chopstick or thin-handled wooden spoon to the side of each potato. Thinly slice the potatoes crosswise, letting the chopstick or spoon handle stop the blade of your knife, and stop ½ inch short of each end of the potato. Rub the potatoes with 1 tablespoon of the olive oil and season with salt and pepper. 2. Place the potatoes, cut-side up, in the air fryer and air fry at 192ºC until golden brown and crisp on the outside and tender inside, about 40 minutes, drizzling the insides with 1 tablespoon more olive oil and seasoning with more salt and pepper halfway through. 3. Meanwhile, in a small blender or food processor, combine the remaining 3 tablespoons olive oil, the chives, parsley, walnuts, Parmesan, lemon juice, and garlic and purée until smooth. Season the chive pesto with salt and pepper. 4. Remove the potatoes from the air fryer and transfer to plates. Drizzle the potatoes with the pesto, letting it drip down into the grooves, then dollop each with sour cream and serve hot.

Glazed Carrots

Prep time: 10 minutes | Cook time: 8 to 10 minutes | Serves 4

2 teaspoons honey
1 teaspoon orange juice
½ teaspoon grated orange zest
⅛ teaspoon ginger

450 g baby carrots
2 teaspoons olive oil
¼ teaspoon salt

1. Combine honey, orange juice, grated rind, and ginger in a small bowl and set aside. 2. Toss the carrots, oil, and salt together to coat well and pour them into the air fryer basket. 3. Roast at 200ºC for 5 minutes. Shake basket to stir a little and cook for 2 to 4 minutes more, until carrots are barely tender. 4. Pour carrots into a baking pan. 5. Stir the honey mixture to combine well, pour glaze over carrots, and stir to coat. 6. Roast at 180ºC for 1 minute or just until heated through.

Charred Okra with Peanut-Chilli Sauce

Prep time: 10 minutes | Cook time: 16 minutes | Serves 2

340 g okra pods
2 tablespoons vegetable oil
Kosher or coarse sea salt and freshly ground black pepper, to taste
1 large shallot, minced
1 garlic clove, minced
½ Scotch bonnet chilli, minced

(deseeded if you want a milder sauce)
1 tablespoon tomato paste
250 ml vegetable stock or water
2 tablespoons natural peanut butter
Juice of ½ lime

1. In a bowl, toss the okra with 1 tablespoon of the oil and season with salt and pepper. Transfer the okra to the air fryer and air fry at 204ºC, shaking the basket halfway through, until the okra is tender and lightly charred at the edges, about 16 minutes. 2. Meanwhile, in a small skillet, heat the remaining 1 tablespoon oil over medium-high heat. Add the shallot, garlic, and chilli and cook, stirring, until soft, about 2 minutes. Stir in the tomato paste and cook for 30 seconds, then stir in the vegetable stock and peanut butter. Reduce the heat to maintain a simmer and cook until the sauce is reduced slightly and thickened, 3 to 4 minutes. Remove the sauce from the heat, stir in the lime juice, and season with salt and pepper. 3. Place the peanut sauce on a plate, then pile the okra on top and serve hot.

Roasted Aubergine

Prep time: 15 minutes | Cook time: 15 minutes | Serves 4

1 large aubergine
2 tablespoons olive oil

¼ teaspoon salt
½ teaspoon garlic powder

1. Remove top and bottom from aubergine. Slice aubergine into ¼-inch-thick round slices. 2. Brush slices with olive oil. Sprinkle with salt and garlic powder. Place aubergine slices into the air fryer basket. 3. Adjust the temperature to 200ºC and set the timer for 15 minutes. 4. Serve immediately.

Fried Asparagus

Prep time: 5 minutes | Cook time: 12 minutes | Serves 4

1 tablespoon olive oil
450 g asparagus spears, ends trimmed
¼ teaspoon salt

¼ teaspoon ground black pepper
1 tablespoon salted butter, melted

1. In a large bowl, drizzle olive oil over asparagus spears and sprinkle with salt and pepper. 2. Place spears into ungreased air fryer basket. Adjust the temperature to 192ºC and set the timer for 12 minutes, shaking the basket halfway through cooking. Asparagus will be lightly browned and tender when done. 3. Transfer to a large dish and drizzle with butter. Serve warm.

Chapter 4 Poultry

Chapter 4 Poultry

Peanut Butter Chicken Satay

Prep time: 12 minutes | Cook time: 12 to 18 minutes | Serves 4

125 g crunchy peanut butter
85 ml chicken stock
3 tablespoons low-sodium soy sauce
2 tablespoons freshly squeezed lemon juice

2 garlic cloves, minced
2 tablespoons extra-virgin olive oil
1 teaspoon curry powder
450 g chicken breast fillets
Cooking oil spray

1. In a medium bowl, whisk the peanut butter, broth, soy sauce, lemon juice, garlic, olive oil, and curry powder until smooth. 2. Place 2 tablespoons of this mixture into a small bowl. Transfer the remaining sauce to a serving bowl and set aside. 3. Add the chicken fillets to the bowl with the 2 tablespoons of sauce and stir to coat. Let stand for a few minutes to marinate. 4. Insert the crisper plate into the basket and the basket into the unit. Preheat the unit by selecting AIR FRY, setting the temperature to 200ºC, and setting the time to 3 minutes. Select START/STOP to begin. 5. Run a 6-inch bamboo skewer lengthwise through each chicken fillet. 6. Once the unit is preheated, spray the crisper plate with cooking oil. Working in batches, place half the chicken skewers into the basket in a single layer without overlapping. 7. Select AIR FRY, set the temperature to 200ºC, and set the time to 9 minutes. Select START/STOP to begin. 8. After 6 minutes, check the chicken. If a food thermometer inserted into the chicken registers 72ºC, it is done. If not, resume cooking. 9. Repeat steps 6, 7, and 8 with the remaining chicken. 10. When the cooking is complete, serve the chicken with the reserved sauce.

Chicken Thighs with Cilantro

Prep time: 15 minutes | Cook time: 25 minutes | Serves 4

1 tablespoon olive oil
Juice of ½ lime
1 tablespoon coconut aminos or tamari
1½ teaspoons Montreal chicken

seasoning
8 bone-in chicken thighs, skin on
2 tablespoons chopped fresh coriander

1. In an extra-large sandwich bag, combine the olive oil, lime juice, coconut aminos, and chicken seasoning. Add the chicken thighs, seal the bag, and massage the bag to ensure the chicken is thoroughly coated. Refrigerate for at least 2 hours, preferably overnight. 2. Preheat the air fryer to 204ºC. 3. Remove the chicken from the marinade (discard the marinade) and arrange in a single layer in the air fryer basket. Pausing halfway through the cooking time to flip the chicken, air fry for 20 to 25 minutes, until a thermometer inserted into the thickest part registers 72ºC. 4. Transfer the chicken to a serving platter and top with the cilantro before serving.

Lemon Chicken

Prep time: 5 minutes | Cook time: 20 to 25 minutes | Serves 4

8 bone-in chicken thighs, skin on
1 tablespoon olive oil
1½ teaspoons lemon-pepper seasoning

½ teaspoon paprika
½ teaspoon garlic powder
¼ teaspoon freshly ground black pepper
Juice of ½ lemon

1. Preheat the air fryer to 180ºC. 2. Place the chicken in a large bowl and drizzle with the olive oil. Top with the lemon-pepper seasoning, paprika, garlic powder, and freshly ground black pepper. Toss until thoroughly coated. 3. Working in batches if necessary, arrange the chicken in a single layer in the basket of the air fryer. Pausing halfway through the cooking time to turn the chicken, air fry for 20 to 25 minutes, until a thermometer inserted into the thickest piece registers 72ºC. 4. Transfer the chicken to a serving platter and squeeze the lemon juice over the top.

Chicken Jalfrezi

Prep time: 15 minutes | Cook time: 15 minutes | Serves 4

Chicken:
450 g boneless, skinless chicken thighs, cut into 2 or 3 pieces each
1 medium onion, chopped
1 large green bell pepper, stemmed, seeded, and chopped
2 tablespoons olive oil
1 teaspoon ground turmeric
1 teaspoon garam masala
1 teaspoon kosher or coarse sea

salt
½ to 1 teaspoon cayenne pepper
Sauce:
60 ml passata
1 tablespoon water
1 teaspoon garam masala
½ teaspoon kosher or coarse sea salt
½ teaspoon cayenne pepper
Side salad, rice, or naan bread, for serving

1. For the chicken: In a large bowl, combine the chicken, onion, bell pepper, oil, turmeric, garam masala, salt, and cayenne. Stir and toss until well combined. 2. Place the chicken and vegetables in the air fryer basket. Set the air fryer to 176ºC for 15 minutes, stirring and tossing halfway through the cooking time. Use a meat thermometer to ensure the chicken has reached an internal temperature of 72ºC. 3. Meanwhile, for the sauce: In a small microwave-safe bowl, combine the tomato sauce, water, garam masala, salt, and cayenne. Microwave on high for 1 minute. Remove and stir. Microwave for another minute; set aside. 4. When the chicken is cooked, remove and place chicken and vegetables in a large bowl. Pour the sauce over all. Stir and toss to coat the chicken and vegetables evenly. 5. Serve with rice, naan, or a side salad.

Italian Chicken Thighs

Prep time: 5 minutes | Cook time: 20 minutes | Serves 2

4 bone-in, skin-on chicken thighs
2 tablespoons unsalted butter, melted
1 teaspoon dried parsley
1 teaspoon dried basil
½ teaspoon garlic powder
¼ teaspoon onion powder
¼ teaspoon dried oregano

1. Brush chicken thighs with butter and sprinkle remaining ingredients over thighs. Place thighs into the air fryer basket. 2. Adjust the temperature to 192ºC and roast for 20 minutes. 3. Halfway through the cooking time, flip the thighs. 4. When fully cooked, internal temperature will be at least 72ºC and skin will be crispy. Serve warm.

Chicken with Bacon and Tomato

Prep time: 25 minutes | Cook time: 10 minutes | Serves 4

4 medium-sized skin-on chicken drumsticks
1½ teaspoons Herbes de Provence
Salt and pepper, to taste
1 tablespoon rice vinegar
2 tablespoons olive oil
2 garlic cloves, crushed
340 g crushed canned tomatoes
1 small-sized leek, thinly sliced
2 slices smoked bacon, chopped

1. Sprinkle the chicken drumsticks with Herbes de Provence, salt and pepper; then drizzle them with rice vinegar and olive oil. 2. Cook in the baking pan at 180ºC for 8 to 10 minutes. Pause the air fryer; stir in the remaining ingredients and continue to cook for 15 minutes longer; make sure to check them periodically. Bon appétit!

Chicken Cordon Bleu

Prep time: 20 minutes | Cook time: 15 to 20 minutes | Serves 4

4 small boneless, skinless chicken breasts
Salt and pepper, to taste
4 slices deli ham
4 slices deli Swiss cheese (about
3 to 4 inches square)
2 tablespoons olive oil
2 teaspoons marjoram
¼ teaspoon paprika

1. Split each chicken breast horizontally almost in two, leaving one edge intact. 2. Lay breasts open flat and sprinkle with salt and pepper to taste. 3. Place a ham slice on top of each chicken breast. 4. Cut cheese slices in half and place one half atop each breast. Set aside remaining halves of cheese slices. 5. Roll up chicken breasts to enclose cheese and ham and secure with toothpicks. 6. Mix together the olive oil, marjoram, and paprika. Rub all over outsides of chicken breasts. 7. Place chicken in air fryer basket and air fry at 180ºC for 15 to 20 minutes, until well done and juices run clear. 8. Remove all toothpicks. To avoid burns, place chicken breasts on a plate to remove toothpicks, then immediately return them to the air fryer basket. 9. Place a half cheese slice on top of each chicken breast and cook for a minute or so just to melt cheese.

Cilantro Lime Chicken Thighs

Prep time: 15 minutes | Cook time: 22 minutes | Serves 4

4 bone-in, skin-on chicken thighs
1 teaspoon baking powder
½ teaspoon garlic powder
2 teaspoons chilli powder
1 teaspoon cumin
2 medium limes
5 g chopped fresh coriander

1. Pat chicken thighs dry and sprinkle with baking powder. 2. In a small bowl, mix garlic powder, chilli powder, and cumin and sprinkle evenly over thighs, gently rubbing on and under chicken skin. 3. Cut one lime in half and squeeze juice over thighs. Place chicken into the air fryer basket. 4. Adjust the temperature to 192ºC and roast for 22 minutes. 5. Cut other lime into four wedges for serving and garnish cooked chicken with wedges and cilantro.

Tex-Mex Chicken Breasts

Prep time: 10 minutes | Cook time: 17 to 20 minutes | Serves 4

450 g boneless, skinless chicken breasts, cut into 1-inch cubes
1 medium onion, chopped
1 red bell pepper, chopped
1 jalapeño pepper, minced
2 teaspoons olive oil
80 g canned black beans, rinsed and drained
125 g salsa
2 teaspoons chilli powder

1. Preheat the air fryer to 204ºC. 2. In a medium metal bowl, mix the chicken, onion, bell pepper, jalapeño, and olive oil. Roast for 10 minutes, stirring once during cooking. 3. Add the black beans, salsa, and chilli powder. Roast for 7 to 10 minutes more, stirring once, until the chicken reaches an internal temperature of 72ºC on a meat thermometer. Serve immediately.

Hawaiian Chicken Bites

Prep time: 1 hour 15 minutes | Cook time: 15 minutes | Serves 4

125 ml pineapple juice
2 tablespoons apple cider vinegar
½ tablespoon minced ginger
125 g ketchup
2 garlic cloves, minced
60 g brown sugar
2 tablespoons sherry or red wine vinegar
125 ml soy sauce
4 chicken breasts, cubed
Cooking spray

1. Combine the pineapple juice, cider vinegar, ginger, ketchup, garlic, and sugar in a saucepan. Stir to mix well. Heat over low heat for 5 minutes or until thickened. Fold in the sherry and soy sauce. 2. Dunk the chicken cubes in the mixture. Press to submerge. Wrap the bowl in plastic and refrigerate to marinate for at least an hour. 3. Preheat the air fryer to 180ºC. Spritz the air fryer basket with cooking spray. 4. Remove the chicken cubes from the marinade. Shake the excess off and put in the preheated air fryer. Spritz with cooking spray. 5. Air fry for 15 minutes or until the chicken cubes are glazed and well browned. Shake the basket at least three times during the frying. 6. Serve immediately.

Italian Crispy Chicken

Prep time: 10 minutes | Cook time: 20 minutes | Serves 4

2 (115 g) boneless, skinless chicken breasts
2 egg whites, beaten
125 g Italian bread crumbs
60 g grated Parmesan cheese
2 teaspoons Italian seasoning
Salt and freshly ground black

pepper, to taste
Cooking oil spray
190 g ready-made marinara sauce
60 g shredded Mozzarella cheese

1. With your knife blade parallel to the cutting board, cut the chicken breasts in half horizontally to create 4 thin cutlets. On a solid surface, pound the cutlets to flatten them. You can use your hands, a rolling pin, a kitchen mallet, or a meat hammer. 2. Pour the egg whites into a bowl large enough to dip the chicken. 3. In another bowl large enough to dip a chicken cutlet in, stir together the bread crumbs, Parmesan cheese, and Italian seasoning, and season with salt and pepper. 4. Dip each cutlet into the egg whites and into the breadcrumb mixture to coat. 5. Insert the crisper plate into the basket and the basket into the unit. Preheat the unit by selecting AIR FRY, setting the temperature to 192°C, and setting the time to 3 minutes. Select START/STOP to begin. 6. Once the unit is preheated, spray the crisper plate with cooking oil. Working in batches, place 2 chicken cutlets into the basket. Spray the top of the chicken with cooking oil. 7. Select AIR FRY, set the temperature to 192°C, and set the time to 7 minutes. Select START/STOP to begin. 8. When the cooking is complete, repeat steps 6 and 7 with the remaining cutlets. 9. Top the chicken cutlets with the marinara sauce and shredded Mozzarella cheese. If the chicken will fit into the basket without stacking, you can prepare all 4 at once. Otherwise, do this 2 cutlets at a time. 10. Select AIR FRY, set the temperature to 192°C, and set the time to 3 minutes. Select START/STOP to begin. 11. The cooking is complete when the cheese is melted and the chicken reaches an internal temperature of 72°C. Cool for 5 minutes before serving.

Chicken and Vegetable Fajitas

Prep time: 15 minutes | Cook time: 23 minutes | Serves 6

Chicken:
450 g boneless, skinless chicken thighs, cut crosswise into thirds
1 tablespoon vegetable oil
4½ teaspoons taco seasoning
Vegetables:
125 g sliced onion
125 g sliced bell pepper
1 or 2 jalapeños, quartered lengthwise

1 tablespoon vegetable oil
½ teaspoon kosher or coarse sea salt
½ teaspoon ground cumin
For Serving:
Tortillas
Sour cream
Shredded cheese
Guacamole
Salsa

1. For the chicken: In a medium bowl, toss together the chicken, vegetable oil, and taco seasoning to coat. 2. For the vegetables: In a separate bowl, toss together the onion, bell pepper, jalapeño(s), vegetable oil, salt, and cumin to coat. 3. Place the chicken in the air fryer basket. Set the air fryer to 192°C for 10 minutes. Add the vegetables to the basket, toss everything together to blend the seasonings, and set the air fryer for 13 minutes more. Use a meat thermometer to ensure the chicken has reached an internal temperature of 72°C. 4. Transfer the chicken and vegetables to a serving platter. Serve with tortillas and the desired fajita fixings.

Ham & Chicken with Cheese

Prep time: 15 minutes | Cook time: 25 minutes | Serves 4

60 g unsalted butter, softened
115 g cream cheese, softened
1½ teaspoons Dijon mustard
2 tablespoons white wine vinegar

60 ml water
250 g shredded cooked chicken
115 g ham, chopped
115 g sliced Swiss or Provolone cheese

1. Preheat the air fryer to 192°C. Lightly coat a casserole dish that will fit in the air fryer, such as an 8-inch round pan, with olive oil and set aside. 2. In a large bowl and using an electric mixer, combine the butter, cream cheese, Dijon mustard, and vinegar. With the motor running at low speed, slowly add the water and beat until smooth. Set aside. 3. Arrange an even layer of chicken in the bottom of the prepared pan, followed by the ham. Spread the butter and cream cheese mixture on top of the ham, followed by the cheese slices on the top layer. Air fry for 20 to 25 minutes until warmed through and the cheese has browned.

Classic Chicken Kebab

Prep time: 35 minutes | Cook time: 25 minutes | Serves 4

60 ml olive oil
1 teaspoon garlic powder
1 teaspoon onion powder
1 teaspoon ground cumin
½ teaspoon dried oregano
½ teaspoon dried basil
60 ml lemon juice
1 tablespoon apple cider vinegar
Olive oil cooking spray

450 g boneless skinless chicken thighs, cut into 1-inch pieces
1 red bell pepper, cut into 1-inch pieces
1 red onion, cut into 1-inch pieces
1 courgette, cut into 1-inch pieces
12 cherry tomatoes

1. In a large bowl, mix together the olive oil, garlic powder, onion powder, cumin, oregano, basil, lemon juice, and apple cider vinegar. 2. Spray six skewers with olive oil cooking spray. 3. On each skewer, slide on a piece of chicken, then a piece of bell pepper, onion, courgette, and finally a tomato and then repeat. Each skewer should have at least two pieces of each item. 4. Once all of the skewers are prepared, place them in a 9-by-13-inch baking dish and pour the olive oil marinade over the top of the skewers. Turn each skewer so that all sides of the chicken and vegetables are coated. 5. Cover the dish with plastic wrap and place it in the refrigerator for 30 minutes. 6. After 30 minutes, preheat the air fryer to 192°C. (If using a grill attachment, make sure it is inside the air fryer during preheating.) 7. Remove the skewers from the marinade and lay them in a single layer in the air fryer basket. If the air fryer has a grill attachment, you can also lay them on this instead. 8. Cook for 10 minutes. Rotate the kebabs, then cook them for 15 minutes more. 9. Remove the skewers from the air fryer and let them rest for 5 minutes before serving.

Curried Orange Honey Chicken

Prep time: 10 minutes | Cook time: 16 to 19 minutes | Serves 4

340 g boneless, skinless chicken thighs, cut into 1-inch pieces
1 yellow bell pepper, cut into 1½-inch pieces
1 small red onion, sliced
Olive oil for misting
60 ml chicken stock
2 tablespoons honey
60 ml orange juice
1 tablespoon cornflour
2 to 3 teaspoons curry powder

1. Preheat the air fryer to 188°C. 2. Put the chicken thighs, pepper, and red onion in the air fryer basket and mist with olive oil. 3. Roast for 12 to 14 minutes or until the chicken is cooked to 72°C, shaking the basket halfway through cooking time. 4. Remove the chicken and vegetables from the air fryer basket and set aside. 5. In a metal bowl, combine the stock, honey, orange juice, cornflour, and curry powder, and mix well. Add the chicken and vegetables, stir, and put the bowl in the basket. 6. Return the basket to the air fryer and roast for 2 minutes. Remove and stir, then roast for 2 to 3 minutes or until the sauce is thickened and bubbly. 7. Serve warm.

Pomegranate Glazed Chicken with Couscous Salad

Prep time: 25 minutes | Cook time: 20 minutes | Serves 4

3 tablespoons plus 2 teaspoons pomegranate molasses
½ teaspoon ground cinnamon
1 teaspoon minced fresh thyme
Salt and ground black pepper, to taste
2 (340 g) bone-in split chicken breasts, trimmed
60 ml chicken broth
60 ml water
60 g couscous
1 tablespoon minced fresh parsley
60 g cherry tomatoes, quartered
1 spring onion, white part minced, green part sliced thin on bias
1 tablespoon extra-virgin olive oil
30 g feta cheese, crumbled
Cooking spray

1. Preheat the air fryer to 176°C. Spritz the air fryer basket with cooking spray. 2. Combine 3 tablespoons of pomegranate molasses, cinnamon, thyme, and ⅛ teaspoon of salt in a small bowl. Stir to mix well. Set aside. 3. Place the chicken breasts in the preheated air fryer, skin side down, and spritz with cooking spray. Sprinkle with salt and ground black pepper. 4. Air fry the chicken for 10 minutes, then brush the chicken with half of pomegranate molasses mixture and flip. Air fry for 5 more minutes. 5. Brush the chicken with remaining pomegranate molasses mixture and flip. Air fry for another 5 minutes or until the internal temperature of the chicken breasts reaches at least 72°C. 6. Meanwhile, pour the broth and water in a pot and bring to a boil over medium-high heat. Add the couscous and sprinkle with salt. Cover and simmer for 7 minutes or until the liquid is almost absorbed. 7. Combine the remaining ingredients, except for the cheese, with cooked couscous in a large bowl. Toss to mix well. Scatter with the feta cheese. 8. When the air frying is complete, remove the chicken from the air fryer and allow to cool for 10 minutes. Serve with vegetable and couscous salad.

Jerk Chicken Thighs

Prep time: 30 minutes | Cook time: 15 to 20 minutes | Serves 6

2 teaspoons ground coriander
1 teaspoon ground allspice
1 teaspoon cayenne pepper
1 teaspoon ground ginger
1 teaspoon salt
1 teaspoon dried thyme
½ teaspoon ground cinnamon
½ teaspoon ground nutmeg
910 g boneless chicken thighs, skin on
2 tablespoons olive oil

1. In a small bowl, combine the coriander, allspice, cayenne, ginger, salt, thyme, cinnamon, and nutmeg. Stir until thoroughly combined. 2. Place the chicken in a baking dish and use paper towels to pat dry. Thoroughly coat both sides of the chicken with the spice mixture. Cover and refrigerate for at least 2 hours, preferably overnight. 3. Preheat the air fryer to 180°C. 4. Working in batches if necessary, arrange the chicken in a single layer in the air fryer basket and lightly coat with the olive oil. Pausing halfway through the cooking time to flip the chicken, air fry for 15 to 20 minutes, until a thermometer inserted into the thickest part registers 72°C.

Nashville Hot Chicken

Prep time: 20 minutes | Cook time: 24 to 28 minutes | Serves 8

1.4 kg bone-in, skin-on chicken pieces, breasts halved crosswise
1 tablespoon sea salt
1 tablespoon freshly ground black pepper
185 g finely ground blanched almond flour
185 g grated Parmesan cheese
1 tablespoon baking powder
2 teaspoons garlic powder, divided
125 g heavy (whipping) cream
2 large eggs, beaten
1 tablespoon vinegar-based hot sauce
Avocado oil spray
125 g (1 stick) unsalted butter
125 ml avocado oil
1 tablespoon cayenne pepper (more or less to taste)
2 tablespoons granulated sweetener

1. Sprinkle the chicken with the salt and pepper. 2. In a large shallow bowl, whisk together the almond flour, Parmesan cheese, baking powder, and 1 teaspoon of the garlic powder. 3. In a separate bowl, whisk together the heavy cream, eggs, and hot sauce. 4. Dip the chicken pieces in the egg, then coat each with the almond flour mixture, pressing the mixture into the chicken to adhere. Allow to sit for 15 minutes to let the breading set. 5. Set the air fryer to 204°C. Place the chicken in a single layer in the air fryer basket, being careful not to overcrowd the pieces, working in batches if necessary. Spray the chicken with oil and roast for 13 minutes. 6. Carefully flip the chicken and spray it with more oil. Reduce the air fryer temperature to 176°C. Roast for another 11 to 15 minutes, until an instant-read thermometer reads 72°C. 7. While the chicken cooks, heat the butter, avocado oil, cayenne pepper, Swerve, and remaining 1 teaspoon of garlic powder in a saucepan over medium-low heat. Cook until the butter is melted and the sugar substitute has dissolved. 8. Remove the chicken from the air fryer. Use tongs to dip the chicken in the sauce. Place the coated chicken on a rack over a baking sheet, and allow it to rest for 5 minutes before serving.

Herb-Buttermilk Chicken Breast

Prep time: 5 minutes | Cook time: 40 minutes | Serves 2

1 large bone-in, skin-on chicken breast
250 ml buttermilk
1½ teaspoons dried parsley
1½ teaspoons dried chives
¾ teaspoon kosher or coarse sea
salt
½ teaspoon dried dill
½ teaspoon onion powder
¼ teaspoon garlic powder
¼ teaspoon dried tarragon
Cooking spray

1. Place the chicken breast in a bowl and pour over the buttermilk, turning the chicken in it to make sure it's completely covered. Let the chicken stand at room temperature for at least 20 minutes or in the refrigerator for up to 4 hours. 2. Meanwhile, in a bowl, stir together the parsley, chives, salt, dill, onion powder, garlic powder, and tarragon. 3. Preheat the air fryer to 148°C. 4. Remove the chicken from the buttermilk, letting the excess drip off, then place the chicken skin-side up directly in the air fryer. Sprinkle the seasoning mix all over the top of the chicken breast, then let stand until the herb mix soaks into the buttermilk, at least 5 minutes. 5. Spray the top of the chicken with cooking spray. Bake for 10 minutes, then increase the temperature to 176°C and bake until an instant-read thermometer inserted into the thickest part of the breast reads 72°C and the chicken is deep golden brown, 30 to 35 minutes. 6. Transfer the chicken breast to a cutting board, let rest for 10 minutes, then cut the meat off the bone and cut into thick slices for serving.

Chicken Paillard

Prep time: 10 minutes | Cook time: 10 minutes | Serves 2

2 large eggs, room temperature
1 tablespoon water
40 g powdered Parmesan cheese
2 teaspoons dried thyme leaves
1 teaspoon ground black pepper
2 (140 g) boneless, skinless chicken breasts, pounded to ½ inch thick
Lemon Butter Sauce:
2 tablespoons unsalted butter, melted
2 teaspoons lemon juice
¼ teaspoon finely chopped fresh thyme leaves, plus more for garnish
⅛ teaspoon fine sea salt
Lemon slices, for serving

1. Spray the air fryer basket with avocado oil. Preheat the air fryer to 200°C. 2. Beat the eggs in a shallow dish, then add the water and stir well. 3. In a separate shallow dish, mix together the Parmesan, thyme, and pepper until well combined. 4. One at a time, dip the chicken breasts in the eggs and let any excess drip off, then dredge both sides of the chicken in the Parmesan mixture. As you finish, set the coated chicken in the air fryer basket. 5. Roast the chicken in the air fryer for 5 minutes, then flip the chicken and cook for another 5 minutes, or until cooked through and the internal temperature reaches 72°C. 6. While the chicken cooks, make the lemon butter sauce: In a small bowl, mix together all the sauce ingredients until well combined. 7. Plate the chicken and pour the sauce over it. Garnish with chopped fresh thyme and serve with lemon slices. 8. Store leftovers in an airtight container in the refrigerator for up to 4 days. Reheat in a preheated 200°C air fryer for 5 minutes, or until heated through.

Turkish Chicken Kebabs

Prep time: 30 minutes | Cook time: 15 minutes | Serves 4

60 g plain Greek yogurt
1 tablespoon minced garlic
1 tablespoon tomato paste
1 tablespoon fresh lemon juice
1 tablespoon vegetable oil
1 teaspoon kosher or coarse sea salt
1 teaspoon ground cumin
1 teaspoon sweet Hungarian paprika
½ teaspoon ground cinnamon
½ teaspoon black pepper
½ teaspoon cayenne pepper
450 g boneless, skinless chicken thighs, quartered crosswise

1. In a large bowl, combine the yogurt, garlic, tomato paste, lemon juice, vegetable oil, salt, cumin, paprika, cinnamon, black pepper, and cayenne. Stir until the spices are blended into the yogurt. 2. Add the chicken to the bowl and toss until well coated. Marinate at room temperature for 30 minutes, or cover and refrigerate for up to 24 hours. 3. Arrange the chicken in a single layer in the air fryer basket. Set the air fryer to 192°C for 10 minutes. Turn the chicken and cook for 5 minutes more. Use a meat thermometer to ensure the chicken has reached an internal temperature of 72°C.

Chicken Legs with Leeks

Prep time: 30 minutes | Cook time: 18 minutes | Serves 6

2 leeks, sliced
2 large-sized tomatoes, chopped
3 cloves garlic, minced
½ teaspoon dried oregano
6 chicken legs, boneless and
skinless
½ teaspoon smoked cayenne pepper
2 tablespoons olive oil
A freshly ground nutmeg

1. In a mixing dish, thoroughly combine all ingredients, minus the leeks. Place in the refrigerator and let it marinate overnight. 2. Lay the leeks onto the bottom of the air fryer basket. Top with the chicken legs. 3. Roast chicken legs at 192°C for 18 minutes, turning halfway through. Serve with hoisin sauce.

Bell Pepper Stuffed Chicken Roll-Ups

Prep time: 10 minutes | Cook time: 12 minutes | Serves 4

2 (115 g) boneless, skinless chicken breasts, slice in half horizontally
1 tablespoon olive oil
Juice of ½ lime
2 tablespoons taco seasoning
½ green bell pepper, cut into strips
½ red bell pepper, cut into strips
¼ onion, sliced

1. Preheat the air fryer to 204°C. 2. Unfold the chicken breast slices on a clean work surface. Rub with olive oil, then drizzle with lime juice and sprinkle with taco seasoning. 3. Top the chicken slices with equal amount of bell peppers and onion. Roll them up and secure with toothpicks. 4. Arrange the chicken roll-ups in the preheated air fryer. Air fry for 12 minutes or until the internal temperature of the chicken reaches at least 72°C. Flip the chicken roll-ups halfway through. 5. Remove the chicken from the air fryer. Discard the toothpicks and serve immediately.

Bacon-Wrapped Chicken Breasts Rolls

Prep time: 10 minutes | Cook time: 15 minutes | Serves 4

5 g chopped fresh chives
2 tablespoons lemon juice
1 teaspoon dried sage
1 teaspoon fresh rosemary leaves
10 g fresh parsley leaves
4 cloves garlic, peeled
1 teaspoon ground fennel
3 teaspoons sea salt
½ teaspoon red pepper flakes
4 (115 g) boneless, skinless chicken breasts, pounded to ¼ inch thick
8 slices bacon
Sprigs of fresh rosemary, for garnish
Cooking spray

1. Preheat the air fryer to 172°C. Spritz the air fryer basket with cooking spray. 2. Put the chives, lemon juice, sage, rosemary, parsley, garlic, fennel, salt, and red pepper flakes in a food processor, then pulse to purée until smooth. 3. Unfold the chicken breasts on a clean work surface, then brush the top side of the chicken breasts with the sauce. 4. Roll the chicken breasts up from the shorter side, then wrap each chicken rolls with 2 bacon slices to cover. Secure with toothpicks. 5. Arrange the rolls in the preheated air fryer, then cook for 10 minutes. Flip the rolls halfway through. 6. Increase the heat to 200°C and air fry for 5 more minutes or until the bacon is browned and crispy. 7. Transfer the rolls to a large plate. Discard the toothpicks and spread with rosemary sprigs before serving.

Piri-Piri Chicken Thighs

Prep time: 5 minutes | Cook time: 25 minutes | Serves 4

60 ml piri-piri sauce
1 tablespoon freshly squeezed lemon juice
2 tablespoons brown sugar, divided
2 cloves garlic, minced
1 tablespoon extra-virgin olive oil
4 bone-in, skin-on chicken thighs, each weighing approximately 198 to 230 g
½ teaspoon cornflour

1. To make the marinade, whisk together the piri-piri sauce, lemon juice, 1 tablespoon of brown sugar, and the garlic in a small bowl. While whisking, slowly pour in the oil in a steady stream and continue to whisk until emulsified. Using a skewer, poke holes in the chicken thighs and place them in a small glass dish. Pour the marinade over the chicken and turn the thighs to coat them with the sauce. Cover the dish and refrigerate for at least 15 minutes and up to 1 hour. 2. Preheat the air fryer to 192°C. Remove the chicken thighs from the dish, reserving the marinade, and place them skin-side down in the air fryer basket. Air fry until the internal temperature reaches 72°C, 15 to 20 minutes. 3. Meanwhile, whisk the remaining brown sugar and the cornflour into the marinade and microwave it on high power for 1 minute until it is bubbling and thickened to a glaze. 4. Once the chicken is cooked, turn the thighs over and brush them with the glaze. Air fry for a few additional minutes until the glaze browns and begins to char in spots. 5. Remove the chicken to a platter and serve with additional piri-piri sauce, if desired.

Herbed Roast Chicken Breast

Prep time: 10 minutes | Cook time: 25 minutes | Serves 2 to 4

2 tablespoons salted butter or ghee, at room temperature
1 teaspoon dried Italian seasoning, crushed
½ teaspoon kosher or coarse sea salt
½ teaspoon smoked paprika
¼ teaspoon black pepper
2 bone-in, skin-on chicken breast halves (280 g each)
Lemon wedges, for serving

1. In a small bowl, stir together the butter, Italian seasoning, salt, paprika, and pepper until thoroughly combined. 2. Using a small sharp knife, carefully loosen the skin on each chicken breast half, starting at the thin end of each. Very carefully separate the skin from the flesh, leaving the skin attached at the thick end of each breast. Divide the herb butter into quarters. Rub one-quarter of the butter onto the flesh of each breast. Fold and lightly press the skin back onto each breast. Rub the remaining butter onto the skin of each breast. 3. Place the chicken in the air fryer basket. Set the air fryer to 192°C for 25 minutes. Use a meat thermometer to ensure the chicken breasts have reached an internal temperature of 72°C. 4. Transfer the chicken to a cutting board. Lightly cover with aluminum foil and let rest for 5 to 10 minutes. 5. Serve with lemon wedges.

Fried Chicken Breasts

Prep time: 30 minutes | Cook time: 12 to 14 minutes | Serves 4

450 g boneless, skinless chicken breasts
190 ml dill pickle juice
95 g finely ground blanched almond flour
95 g finely grated Parmesan
cheese
½ teaspoon sea salt
½ teaspoon freshly ground black pepper
2 large eggs
Avocado oil spray

1. Place the chicken breasts in a sandwich bag or between two pieces of cling film. Using a meat mallet or heavy skillet, pound the chicken to a uniform ½-inch thickness. 2. Place the chicken in a large bowl with the pickle juice. Cover and allow to brine in the refrigerator for up to 2 hours. 3. In a shallow dish, combine the almond flour, Parmesan cheese, salt, and pepper. In a separate, shallow bowl, beat the eggs. 4. Drain the chicken and pat it dry with paper towels. Dip in the eggs and then in the flour mixture, making sure to press the coating into the chicken. Spray both sides of the coated breasts with oil. 5. Spray the air fryer basket with oil and put the chicken inside. Set the temperature to 204°C and air fry for 6 to 7 minutes. 6. Carefully flip the breasts with a spatula. Spray the breasts again with oil and continue cooking for 6 to 7 minutes more, until golden and crispy.

Chicken Schnitzel Dogs

Prep time: 15 minutes | Cook time: 8 to 10 minutes | Serves 4

60 g plain flour
½ teaspoon salt
1 teaspoon marjoram
1 teaspoon dried parsley flakes
½ teaspoon thyme
1 egg
1 teaspoon lemon juice
1 teaspoon water

125 g bread crumbs
4 chicken breast fillets, pounded thin
Oil for misting or cooking spray
4 whole grain hotdog buns
4 slices Gouda cheese
1 small Granny Smith apple, thinly sliced
60 g shredded Savoy cabbage
Coleslaw dressing

1. In a shallow dish, mix together the flour, salt, marjoram, parsley, and thyme. 2. In another shallow dish, beat together egg, lemon juice, and water. 3. Place bread crumbs in a third shallow dish. 4. Cut each of the flattened chicken fillets in half lengthwise. 5. Dip flattened chicken strips in flour mixture, then egg wash. Let excess egg drip off and roll in bread crumbs. Spray both sides with oil or cooking spray. 6. Air fry at 200ºC for 5 minutes. Spray with oil, turn over, and spray other side. 7. Cook for 3 to 5 minutes more, until well done and crispy brown. 8. To serve, place 2 schnitzel strips on bottom of each hotdog bun. Top with cheese, sliced apple, and cabbage. Drizzle with coleslaw dressing and top with other half of bun.

Buffalo Chicken Wings

Prep time: 10 minutes | Cook time: 20 to 25 minutes | Serves 4

2 tablespoons baking powder
1 teaspoon smoked paprika
Sea salt and freshly ground black pepper, to taste
910 g chicken wings or chicken drumsticks
Avocado oil spray

85 ml avocado oil
125 g Buffalo hot sauce, such as Frank's RedHot
4 tablespoons unsalted butter
2 tablespoons apple cider vinegar
1 teaspoon minced garlic

1. In a large bowl, stir together the baking powder, smoked paprika, and salt and pepper to taste. Add the chicken wings and toss to coat. 2. Set the air fryer to 204ºC. Spray the wings with oil. 3. Place the wings in the basket in a single layer, working in batches, and air fry for 20 to 25 minutes. Check with an instant-read thermometer and remove when they reach 68ºC. Let rest until they reach 72ºC. 4. While the wings are cooking, whisk together the avocado oil, hot sauce, butter, vinegar, and garlic in a small saucepan over medium-low heat until warm. 5. When the wings are done cooking, toss them with the Buffalo sauce. Serve warm.

Chapter 5 Fish and Seafood

Chapter 5 Fish and Seafood

Salmon on Bed of Fennel and Carrot

Prep time: 15 minutes | Cook time: 13 to 14 minutes | Serves 2

1 fennel bulb, thinly sliced
1 large carrot, peeled and sliced
1 small onion, thinly sliced
60 g low-fat sour cream
¼ teaspoon coarsely ground pepper
2 (140 g) salmon fillets

1. Combine the fennel, carrot, and onion in a bowl and toss. 2. Put the vegetable mixture into a baking pan. Roast in the air fryer at 204°C for 4 minutes or until the vegetables are crisp-tender. 3. Remove the pan from the air fryer. Stir in the sour cream and sprinkle the vegetables with the pepper. 4. Top with the salmon fillets. 5. Return the pan to the air fryer. Roast for another 9 to 10 minutes or until the salmon just barely flakes when tested with a fork.

Pecan-Crusted Catfish

Prep time: 5 minutes | Cook time: 12 minutes | Serves 4

60 g pecan meal
1 teaspoon fine sea salt
¼ teaspoon ground black pepper
4 (115 g) catfish fillets

For Garnish (Optional):
Fresh oregano
Pecan halves

1. Spray the air fryer basket with avocado oil. Preheat the air fryer to 192°C. 2. In a large bowl, mix the pecan meal, salt, and pepper. One at a time, dredge the catfish fillets in the mixture, coating them well. Use your hands to press the pecan meal into the fillets. Spray the fish with avocado oil and place them in the air fryer basket. 3. Air fry the coated catfish for 12 minutes, or until it flakes easily and is no longer translucent in the center, flipping halfway through. 4. Garnish with oregano sprigs and pecan halves, if desired. 5. Store leftovers in an airtight container in the fridge for up to 3 days. Reheat in a preheated 176°C air fryer for 4 minutes, or until heated through.

Tilapia Almondine

Prep time: 10 minutes | Cook time: 10 minutes | Serves 2

60 g almond flour or fine dried bread crumbs
2 tablespoons salted butter or ghee, melted
1 teaspoon black pepper
½ teaspoon kosher or coarse sea
salt
60 g mayonnaise
2 tilapia fillets
60 g thinly sliced almonds
Vegetable oil spray

1. In a small bowl, mix together the almond flour, butter, pepper and salt. 2. Spread the mayonnaise on both sides of each fish fillet.

Dredge the fillets in the almond flour mixture. Spread the sliced almonds on one side of each fillet, pressing lightly to adhere. 3. Spray the air fryer basket with vegetable oil spray. Place the fish fillets in the basket. Set the air fryer to 164°C for 10 minutes, or until the fish flakes easily with a fork.

Crustless Prawn Quiche

Prep time: 15 minutes | Cook time: 20 minutes | Serves 2

Vegetable oil
4 large eggs
125 ml single cream
115 g raw prawns, chopped
125 g shredded Parmesan or
Swiss cheese
30 g chopped spring onions
1 teaspoon sweet smoked paprika
1 teaspoon Herbes de Provence
1 teaspoon black pepper
½ to 1 teaspoon kosher salt

1. Generously grease a baking pan with vegetable oil. (Be sure to grease the pan well, the proteins in eggs stick something fierce. Alternatively, line the bottom of the pan with baking paper cut to fit and spray the baking paper and sides of the pan generously with vegetable oil spray.) 2. In a large bowl, beat together the eggs and single cream. Add the prawns, 95 g cheese, the spring onions, paprika, Herbes de Provence, pepper, and salt. Stir with a fork to thoroughly combine. Pour the egg mixture into the prepared pan. 3. Place the pan in the air fryer basket. Set the air fryer to 148°C for 20 minutes. After 17 minutes, sprinkle the remaining 30 g cheese on top and cook for the remaining 3 minutes, or until the cheese has melted, the eggs are set, and a toothpick inserted into the center comes out clean. 4. Serve the quiche warm or at room temperature.

Crunchy Fish Sticks

Prep time: 30 minutes | Cook time: 9 minutes | Serves 4

450 g cod fillets
185 g finely ground blanched almond flour
2 teaspoons Old Bay seasoning
½ teaspoon paprika
Sea salt and freshly ground
black pepper, to taste
60 g sugar-free mayonnaise
1 large egg, beaten
Avocado oil spray
Tartar sauce, for serving

1. Cut the fish into ¾-inch-wide strips. 2. In a shallow bowl, stir together the almond flour, Old Bay seasoning, paprika, and salt and pepper to taste. In another shallow bowl, whisk together the mayonnaise and egg. 3. Dip the cod strips in the egg mixture, then the almond flour, gently pressing with your fingers to help adhere to the coating. 4. Place the coated fish on a baking paper-lined baking sheet and freeze for 30 minutes. 5. Spray the air fryer basket with oil. Set the air fryer to 204°C. Place the fish in the basket in a single layer, and spray each piece with oil. 6. Cook for 5 minutes. Flip and spray with more oil. Cook for 4 minutes more, until the internal temperature reaches 60°C. Serve with the tartar sauce.

Prawn Caesar Salad

Prep time: 30 minutes | Cook time: 4 to 6 minutes | Serves 4

340 g fresh large prawns, peeled and deveined
1 tablespoon plus 1 teaspoon freshly squeezed lemon juice, divided
4 tablespoons olive oil or avocado oil, divided
2 garlic cloves, minced, divided
¼ teaspoon sea salt, plus additional to season the

marinade
¼ teaspoon freshly ground black pepper, plus additional to season the marinade
80 g sugar-free mayonnaise
2 tablespoons freshly grated Parmesan cheese
1 teaspoon Dijon mustard
1 tinned anchovy, mashed
340 g romaine hearts, torn

1. Place the prawns in a large bowl. Add 1 tablespoon of lemon juice, 1 tablespoon of olive oil, and 1 minced garlic clove. Season with salt and pepper. Toss well and refrigerate for 15 minutes. 2. While the prawns marinate, make the dressing: In a blender, combine the mayonnaise, Parmesan cheese, Dijon mustard, the remaining 1 teaspoon of lemon juice, the anchovy, the remaining minced garlic clove, ¼ teaspoon of salt, and ¼ teaspoon of pepper. Process until smooth. With the blender running, slowly stream in the remaining 3 tablespoons of oil. Transfer the mixture to a jar; seal and refrigerate until ready to serve. 3. Remove the prawns from its marinade and place it in the air fryer basket in a single layer. Set the air fryer to 204°C and air fry for 2 minutes. Flip the prawn and cook for 2 to 4 minutes more, until the flesh turns opaque. 4. Place the romaine in a large bowl and toss with the desired amount of dressing. Top with the prawns and serve immediately.

Fish Tacos with Jalapeño-Lime Sauce

Prep time: 25 minutes | Cook time: 7 to 10 minutes | Serves 4

Fish Tacos:
450 g fish fillets
¼ teaspoon cumin
¼ teaspoon coriander
⅛ teaspoon ground red pepper
1 tablespoon lime zest
¼ teaspoon smoked paprika
1 teaspoon oil
Cooking spray
6 to 8 corn or flour tortillas (6-inch size)
Jalapeño-Lime Sauce:

125 ml sour cream
1 tablespoon lime juice
¼ teaspoon grated lime zest
½ teaspoon minced jalapeño (flesh only)
¼ teaspoon cumin
Savoy Cabbage Garnish:
125 g shredded Savoy cabbage
30 g slivered red or green bell pepper
30 g slivered onion

1. Slice the fish fillets into strips approximately ½-inch thick. 2. Put the strips into a sealable plastic bag along with the cumin, coriander, red pepper, lime zest, smoked paprika, and oil. Massage seasonings into the fish until evenly distributed. 3. Spray the air fryer basket with nonstick cooking spray and place seasoned fish inside. 4. Air fry at 200°C for approximately 5 minutes. Shake basket to distribute fish. Cook an additional 2 to 5 minutes, until fish flakes easily. 5. While the fish is cooking, prepare the Jalapeño-Lime Sauce by mixing the sour cream, lime juice, lime zest, jalapeño, and cumin together to make a smooth sauce. Set aside. 6. Mix the cabbage, bell pepper, and onion together and set aside. 7. To warm refrigerated tortillas, wrap in damp paper towels and microwave for 30 to 60 seconds. 8. To serve, spoon some of fish into a warm tortilla. Add one or two tablespoons Savoy Cabbage Garnish and drizzle with Jalapeño-Lime Sauce.

Fish Taco Bowl

Prep time: 10 minutes | Cook time: 12 minutes | Serves 4

½ teaspoon salt
¼ teaspoon garlic powder
¼ teaspoon ground cumin
4 (115 g) cod fillets
500 g finely shredded green

cabbage
80 g mayonnaise
¼ teaspoon ground black pepper
30 g chopped pickled jalapeños

1. Sprinkle salt, garlic powder, and cumin over cod and place into ungreased air fryer basket. Adjust the temperature to 176°C and air fry for 12 minutes, turning fillets halfway through cooking. Cod will flake easily and have an internal temperature of at least 64°C when done. 2. In a large bowl, toss cabbage with mayonnaise, pepper, and jalapeños until fully coated. Serve cod warm over cabbage slaw on four medium plates.

Tandoori-Spiced Salmon and Potatoes

Prep time: 10 minutes | Cook time: 28 minutes | Serves 2

450 g fingerling or new potatoes
2 tablespoons vegetable oil, divided
Kosher or coarse sea salt and freshly ground black pepper, to taste

1 teaspoon ground turmeric
1 teaspoon ground cumin
1 teaspoon ground ginger
½ teaspoon smoked paprika
¼ teaspoon cayenne pepper
2 (170 g) skin-on salmon fillets

1. Preheat the air fryer to 192°C. 2. In a bowl, toss the potatoes with 1 tablespoon of the oil until evenly coated. Season with salt and pepper. Transfer the potatoes to the air fryer and air fry for 20 minutes. 3. Meanwhile, in a bowl, combine the remaining 1 tablespoon oil, the turmeric, cumin, ginger, paprika, and cayenne. Add the salmon fillets and turn in the spice mixture until fully coated all over. 4. After the potatoes have cooked for 20 minutes, place the salmon fillets, skin-side up, on top of the potatoes, and continue cooking until the potatoes are tender, the salmon is cooked, and the salmon skin is slightly crisp. 5. Transfer the salmon fillets to two plates and serve with the potatoes while both are warm.

Parmesan Mackerel with Coriander

Prep time: 10 minutes | Cook time: 7 minutes | Serves 2

340 g mackerel fillet
60 g Parmesan, grated

1 teaspoon ground coriander
1 tablespoon olive oil

1. Sprinkle the mackerel fillet with olive oil and put it in the air fryer basket. 2. Top the fish with ground coriander and Parmesan. 3. Cook the fish at 200°C for 7 minutes.

Blackened Fish

Prep time: 15 minutes | Cook time: 8 minutes | Serves 4

1 large egg, beaten
Blackened seasoning, as needed
2 tablespoons light brown sugar

4 (115 g) tilapia fillets
Cooking spray

1. In a shallow bowl, place the beaten egg. In a second shallow bowl, stir together the Blackened seasoning and the brown sugar. 2. One at a time, dip the fish fillets in the egg, then the brown sugar mixture, coating thoroughly. 3. Preheat the air fryer to 148ºC. Line the air fryer basket with baking paper. 4. Place the coated fish on the baking paper and spritz with oil. 5. Bake for 4 minutes. Flip the fish, spritz it with oil, and bake for 4 to 6 minutes more until the fish is white inside and flakes easily with a fork. 6. Serve immediately.

Easy Scallops

Prep time: 5 minutes | Cook time: 4 minutes | Serves 2

12 medium sea scallops, rinsed and patted dry
1 teaspoon fine sea salt
¾ teaspoon ground black

pepper, plus more for garnish
Fresh thyme leaves, for garnish (optional)
Avocado oil spray

1. Preheat the air fryer to 200ºC. Coat the air fryer basket with avocado oil spray. 2. Place the scallops in a medium bowl and spritz with avocado oil spray. Sprinkle the salt and pepper to season. 3. Transfer the seasoned scallops to the air fryer basket, spacing them apart. You may need to work in batches to avoid overcrowding. 4. Air fry for 4 minutes, flipping the scallops halfway through, or until the scallops are firm and reach an internal temperature of just 64ºC on a meat thermometer. 5. Remove from the basket and repeat with the remaining scallops. 6. Sprinkle the pepper and thyme leaves on top for garnish, if desired. Serve immediately.

Moroccan Spiced Halibut with Chickpea Salad

Prep time: 15 minutes | Cook time: 12 minutes | Serves 2

¾ teaspoon ground coriander
½ teaspoon ground cumin
¼ teaspoon ground ginger
⅛ teaspoon ground cinnamon
Salt and pepper, to taste
2 (230 g) skinless halibut fillets, 1¼ inches thick
4 teaspoons extra-virgin olive oil, divided, plus extra for drizzling

1 (425 g) can chickpeas, rinsed
1 tablespoon lemon juice, plus lemon wedges for serving
1 teaspoon harissa
½ teaspoon honey
2 carrots, peeled and shredded
2 tablespoons chopped fresh mint, divided
Vegetable oil spray

1. Preheat the air fryer to 148ºC. 2. Make foil sling for air fryer basket by folding 1 long sheet of aluminum foil so it is 4 inches wide. Lay sheet of foil widthwise across basket, pressing foil into and up sides of basket. Fold excess foil as needed so that edges of foil are flush with top of basket. Lightly spray foil and basket with vegetable oil spray. 3. Combine coriander, cumin, ginger, cinnamon, ⅛ teaspoon salt, and ⅛ teaspoon pepper in a small bowl. Pat halibut dry with paper towels, rub with 1 teaspoon oil, and sprinkle all over with spice mixture. Arrange fillets skinned side down on sling in prepared basket, spaced evenly apart. Bake until halibut flakes apart when gently prodded with a paring knife and registers 60ºC, 12 to 16 minutes, using the sling to rotate fillets halfway through cooking. 4. Meanwhile, microwave chickpeas in medium bowl until heated through, about 2 minutes. Stir in remaining 1 tablespoon oil, lemon juice, harissa, honey, ⅛ teaspoon salt, and ⅛ teaspoon pepper. Add carrots and 1 tablespoon mint and toss to combine. Season with salt and pepper, to taste. 5. Using sling, carefully remove halibut from air fryer and transfer to individual plates. Sprinkle with remaining 1 tablespoon mint and drizzle with extra oil to taste. Serve with salad and lemon wedges.

Dukkah-Crusted Halibut

Prep time: 15 minutes | Cook time: 17 minutes | Serves 2

Dukkah:
1 tablespoon coriander seeds
1 tablespoon sesame seeds
1½ teaspoons cumin seeds
40 g roasted mixed nuts
¼ teaspoon kosher or coarse sea salt

¼ teaspoon black pepper
Fish:
2 (140 g) halibut fillets
2 tablespoons mayonnaise
Vegetable oil spray
Lemon wedges, for serving

1. For the dukkah: Combine the coriander, sesame seeds, and cumin in a small baking pan. Place the pan in the air fryer basket. Set the air fryer to 204ºC for 5 minutes. Toward the end of the cooking time, you will hear the seeds popping. Transfer to a plate and let cool for 5 minutes. 2. Transfer the toasted seeds to a food processor or spice grinder and add the mixed nuts. Pulse until coarsely chopped. Add the salt and pepper and stir well. 3. For the fish: Spread each fillet with 1 tablespoon of the mayonnaise. Press a heaping tablespoon of the dukkah into the mayonnaise on each fillet, pressing lightly to adhere. 4. Spray the air fryer basket with vegetable oil spray. Place the fish in the basket. Set the air fryer to 204ºC for 12 minutes, or until the fish flakes easily with a fork. 5. Serve the fish with lemon wedges.

Golden Prawns

Prep time: 20 minutes | Cook time: 7 minutes | Serves 4

2 egg whites
60 g coconut flour
125 g Parmigiano-Reggiano, grated
½ teaspoon celery seeds
½ teaspoon porcini powder
½ teaspoon onion powder

1 teaspoon garlic powder
½ teaspoon dried rosemary
½ teaspoon sea salt
½ teaspoon ground black pepper
680 g prawns, peeled and deveined

1. Whisk the egg with coconut flour and Parmigiano-Reggiano. Add in seasonings and mix to combine well. 2. Dip your prawns in the batter. Roll until they are covered on all sides. 3. Cook in the preheated air fryer at 200ºC for 5 to 7 minutes or until golden brown. Work in batches. Serve with lemon wedges if desired.

Tuna-Stuffed Tomatoes

Prep time: 5 minutes | Cook time: 5 minutes | Serves 2

2 medium beefsteak tomatoes, tops removed, seeded, membranes removed
2 (75 g) pouches tuna packed in water, drained
1 medium stalk celery, trimmed and chopped
2 tablespoons mayonnaise
¼ teaspoon salt
¼ teaspoon ground black pepper
2 teaspoons coconut oil
30 g shredded mild Cheddar cheese

1. Scoop pulp out of each tomato, leaving ½-inch shell. 2. In a medium bowl, mix tuna, celery, mayonnaise, salt, and pepper. Drizzle with coconut oil. Spoon ½ mixture into each tomato and top each with 2 tablespoons Cheddar. 3. Place tomatoes into ungreased air fryer basket. Adjust the temperature to 160°C and air fry for 5 minutes. Cheese will be melted when done. Serve warm.

BBQ Prawns with Creole Butter Sauce

Prep time: 10 minutes | Cook time: 12 to 15 minutes | Serves 4

6 tablespoons unsalted butter
85 ml Worcestershire sauce
3 cloves garlic, minced
Juice of 1 lemon
1 teaspoon paprika
1 teaspoon Creole seasoning
680 g large uncooked prawns, peeled and deveined
2 tablespoons fresh parsley

1. Preheat the air fryer to 188°C. 2. In a large microwave-safe bowl, combine the butter, Worcestershire, and garlic. Microwave on high for 1 to 2 minutes until the butter is melted. Stir in the lemon juice, paprika, and Creole seasoning. Add the prawns and toss until thoroughly coated. 3. Transfer the mixture to a casserole dish or pan that fits in your air fryer. Pausing halfway through the cooking time to turn the prawns, air fry for 12 to 15 minutes, until the prawns are cooked through. Top with the parsley just before serving.

Bang Bang Prawns

Prep time: 15 minutes | Cook time: 14 minutes | Serves 4

Sauce:
125 g mayonnaise
60 g sweet chilli sauce
2 to 4 tablespoons Sriracha
1 teaspoon minced fresh ginger
Prawns:
450 g jumbo raw prawns (21 to
25 count), peeled and deveined
2 tablespoons cornflour or rice flour
½ teaspoon kosher or coarse sea salt
Vegetable oil spray

1. For the sauce: In a large bowl, combine the mayonnaise, chilli sauce, Sriracha, and ginger. Stir until well combined. Remove half of the sauce to serve as a dipping sauce. 2. For the prawns: Place the prawns in a medium bowl. Sprinkle the cornflour and salt over the prawns and toss until well coated. 3. Place the prawns in the air fryer basket in a single layer. (If they won't fit in a single layer, set a rack or trivet on top of the bottom layer of prawns and place the rest of the prawns on the rack.) Spray generously with vegetable oil spray. Set the air fryer to 176°C for 10 minutes, turning and spraying with additional oil spray halfway through the cooking time. 4. Remove the prawns and toss in the bowl with half of the sauce. Place the prawns back in the air fryer basket. Set the air fryer to 176°C for an additional 4 to 5 minutes, or until the sauce has formed a glaze. 5. Serve the hot prawns with the reserved sauce for dipping.

Asian Swordfish

Prep time: 10 minutes | Cook time: 6 to 11 minutes | Serves 4

4 (115 g) swordfish steaks
½ teaspoon toasted sesame oil
1 jalapeño pepper, finely minced
2 garlic cloves, grated
1 tablespoon grated fresh ginger
½ teaspoon Chinese five-spice
powder
⅛ teaspoon freshly ground black pepper
2 tablespoons freshly squeezed lemon juice

1. Place the swordfish steaks on a work surface and drizzle with the sesame oil. 2. In a small bowl, mix the jalapeño, garlic, ginger, five-spice powder, pepper, and lemon juice. Rub this mixture into the fish and let it stand for 10 minutes. 3. Roast the swordfish in the air fryer at 192°C for 6 to 11 minutes, or until the swordfish reaches an internal temperature of at least 60°C on a meat thermometer. Serve immediately.

Paprika Crab Burgers

Prep time: 30 minutes | Cook time: 14 minutes | Serves 3

2 eggs, beaten
1 shallot, chopped
2 garlic cloves, crushed
1 tablespoon olive oil
1 teaspoon yellow mustard
1 teaspoon fresh coriander,
chopped
280 g crab meat
1 teaspoon smoked paprika
½ teaspoon ground black pepper
Sea salt, to taste
95 g Parmesan cheese

1. In a mixing bowl, thoroughly combine the eggs, shallot, garlic, olive oil, mustard, coriander, crab meat, paprika, black pepper, and salt. Mix until well combined. 2. Shape the mixture into 6 patties. Roll the crab patties over grated Parmesan cheese, coating well on all sides. Place in your refrigerator for 2 hours. 3. Spritz the crab patties with cooking oil on both sides. Cook in the preheated air fryer at 180°C for 14 minutes. Serve on dinner rolls if desired. Bon appétit!

Balsamic Tilapia

Prep time: 5 minutes | Cook time: 15 minutes | Serves 4

4 tilapia fillets, boneless
2 tablespoons balsamic vinegar
1 teaspoon avocado oil
1 teaspoon dried basil

1. Sprinkle the tilapia fillets with balsamic vinegar, avocado oil, and dried basil. 2. Then put the fillets in the air fryer basket and cook at 184°C for 15 minutes.

Honey-Balsamic Salmon

Prep time: 5 minutes | Cook time: 8 minutes | Serves 2

Oil, for spraying
2 (170 g) salmon fillets
60 ml balsamic vinegar
2 tablespoons honey
2 teaspoons red pepper flakes
2 teaspoons olive oil
½ teaspoon salt
¼ teaspoon freshly ground black pepper

1. Line the air fryer basket with baking paper and spray lightly with oil. 2. Place the salmon in the prepared basket. 3. In a small bowl, whisk together the balsamic vinegar, honey, red pepper flakes, olive oil, salt, and black pepper. Brush the mixture over the salmon. 4. Roast at 200°C for 7 to 8 minutes, or until the internal temperature reaches 64°C. Serve immediately.

Tilapia with Pecans

Prep time: 20 minutes | Cook time: 16 minutes | Serves 5

2 tablespoons ground flaxseeds
1 teaspoon paprika
Sea salt and white pepper, to taste
1 teaspoon garlic paste
2 tablespoons extra-virgin olive oil
60 g pecans, ground
5 tilapia fillets, sliced into halves

1. Combine the ground flaxseeds, paprika, salt, white pepper, garlic paste, olive oil, and ground pecans in a sandwich bag. Add the fish fillets and shake to coat well. 2. Spritz the air fryer basket with cooking spray. Cook in the preheated air fryer at 204°C for 10 minutes; turn them over and cook for 6 minutes more. Work in batches. 3. Serve with lemon wedges, if desired. Enjoy!

Pesto Fish Pie

Prep time: 15 minutes | Cook time: 15 minutes | Serves 4

2 tablespoons prepared pesto
60 ml single cream
30 g grated Parmesan cheese
1 teaspoon kosher or coarse sea salt
1 teaspoon black pepper
Vegetable oil spray
280 g frozen chopped spinach,
thawed and squeezed dry
450 g firm white fish, cut into 2-inch chunks
60 g cherry tomatoes, quartered
Plain flour
½ sheet frozen puff pastry (from a 490 g package), thawed

1. In a small bowl, combine the pesto, single cream, Parmesan, salt, and pepper. Stir until well combined; set aside. 2. Spray a baking pan with vegetable oil spray. Arrange the spinach evenly across the bottom of the pan. Top with the fish and tomatoes. Pour the pesto mixture evenly over everything. 3. On a lightly floured surface, roll the puff pastry sheet into a circle. Place the pastry on top of the pan and tuck it in around the edges of the pan. (Or, do what I do and stretch it with your hands and then pat it into place.) 4. Place the pan in the air fryer basket. Set the air fryer to 204°C for 15 minutes, or until the pastry is well browned. Let stand 5 minutes before serving.

Fish Cakes

Prep time: 30 minutes | Cook time: 10 to 12 minutes | Serves 4

95 g mashed potatoes (about 1 large russet potato)
340 g cod or other white fish
Salt and pepper, to taste
Oil for misting or cooking spray
1 large egg
30 g potato starch
60 g panko bread crumbs
1 tablespoon fresh chopped chives
2 tablespoons minced onion

1. Peel potatoes, cut into cubes, and cook on stovetop till soft. 2. Salt and pepper raw fish to taste. Mist with oil or cooking spray, and air fry at 180°C for 6 to 8 minutes, until fish flakes easily. If fish is crowded, rearrange halfway through cooking to ensure all pieces cook evenly. 3. Transfer fish to a plate and break apart to cool. 4. Beat egg in a shallow dish. 5. Place potato starch in another shallow dish, and panko crumbs in a third dish. 6. When potatoes are done, drain in colander and rinse with cold water. 7. In a large bowl, mash the potatoes and stir in the chives and onion. Add salt and pepper to taste, then stir in the fish. 8. If needed, stir in a tablespoon of the beaten egg to help bind the mixture. 9. Shape into 8 small, fat patties. Dust lightly with potato starch, dip in egg, and roll in panko crumbs. Spray both sides with oil or cooking spray. 10. Air fry at 180°C for 10 to 12 minutes, until golden brown and crispy.

Mediterranean-Style Cod

Prep time: 5 minutes | Cook time: 12 minutes | Serves 4

4 (170 g) cod fillets
3 tablespoons fresh lemon juice
1 tablespoon olive oil
¼ teaspoon salt
6 cherry tomatoes, halved
30 g pitted and sliced Kalamata olives

1. Place cod into an ungreased round nonstick baking dish. Pour lemon juice into dish and drizzle cod with olive oil. Sprinkle with salt. Place tomatoes and olives around baking dish in between fillets. 2. Place dish into air fryer basket. Adjust the temperature to 176°C and bake for 12 minutes, carefully turning cod halfway through cooking. Fillets will be lightly browned, easily flake, and have an internal temperature of at least 64°C when done. Serve warm.

Quick Prawn Skewers

Prep time: 10 minutes | Cook time: 5 minutes | Serves 5

1.8 kg prawns, peeled and deveined
1 tablespoon dried rosemary
1 tablespoon avocado oil
1 teaspoon apple cider vinegar

1. Mix the prawns with dried rosemary, avocado oil, and apple cider vinegar. 2. Then sting the prawns into skewers and put in the air fryer. 3. Cook the prawns at 204°C for 5 minutes.

Nutty Prawns with Amaretto Glaze

Prep time: 30 minutes | Cook time: 10 minutes per batch | Serves 10 to 12

125 g plain flour	oil
½ teaspoon baking powder	250 g sliced almonds
1 teaspoon salt	910 g large prawns (about
2 eggs, beaten	32 to 40 prawns), peeled and
125 ml milk	deveined, tails left on
2 tablespoons olive or vegetable	500 ml amaretto liqueur

1. Combine the flour, baking powder and salt in a large bowl. Add the eggs, milk and oil and stir until it forms a smooth batter. Coarsely crush the sliced almonds into a second shallow dish with your hands. 2. Dry the prawns well with paper towels. Dip the prawns into the batter and shake off any excess batter, leaving just enough to lightly coat the prawns. Transfer the prawns to the dish with the almonds and coat completely. Place the coated prawns on a plate or baking sheet and when all the prawns have been coated, freeze them for an 1 hour, or as long as a week before air frying. 3. Preheat the air fryer to 204°C. 4. Transfer 8 frozen prawns at a time to the air fryer basket. Air fry for 6 minutes. Turn the prawns over and air fry for an additional 4 minutes. Repeat with the remaining prawns. 5. While the prawns are cooking, bring the Amaretto to a boil in a small saucepan on the stovetop. Lower the heat and simmer until it has reduced and thickened into a glaze, about 10 minutes. 6. Remove the prawns from the air fryer and brush both sides with the warm amaretto glaze. Serve warm.

Prawn Pasta with Basil and Mushrooms

Prep time: 10 minutes | Cook time: 10 minutes | Serves 6

450 g small prawns, peeled and deveined	230 g baby mushrooms, sliced
80 ml olive oil, divided	60 g Parmesan, plus more for serving (optional)
¼ teaspoon garlic powder	1 teaspoon salt
¼ teaspoon cayenne	½ teaspoon black pepper
450 g whole grain pasta	10 g fresh basil
5 garlic cloves, minced	

1. Preheat the air fryer to 192°C. 2. In a small bowl, combine the prawns, 1 tablespoon olive oil, garlic powder, and cayenne. Toss to coat the prawns. 3. Place the prawns into the air fryer basket and roast for 5 minutes. Remove the prawns and set aside. 4. Cook the pasta according to package directions. Once done cooking, reserve 125 ml pasta water, then drain. 5. Meanwhile, in a large skillet, heat 60 ml olive oil over medium heat. Add the garlic and mushrooms and cook down for 5 minutes. 6. Pour the pasta, reserved pasta water, Parmesan, salt, pepper, and basil into the skillet with the vegetable-and-oil mixture, and stir to coat the pasta. 7. Toss in the prawns and remove from heat, then let the mixture sit for 5 minutes before serving with additional Parmesan, if desired.

Cheesy Tuna Patties

Prep time: 5 minutes | Cook time: 17 to 18 minutes | Serves 4

Tuna Patties:	pepper, to taste
450 g canned tuna, drained	1 tablespoon sesame oil
1 egg, whisked	Cheese Sauce:
2 tablespoons shallots, minced	1 tablespoon butter
1 garlic clove, minced	250 ml beer
125 g grated Romano cheese	2 tablespoons grated Colby
Sea salt and ground black	cheese

1. Mix together the canned tuna, whisked egg, shallots, garlic, cheese, salt, and pepper in a large bowl and stir to incorporate. 2. Divide the tuna mixture into four equal portions and form each portion into a patty with your hands. Refrigerate the patties for 2 hours. 3. When ready, brush both sides of each patty with sesame oil. 4. Preheat the air fryer to 180°C. 5. Place the patties in the air fryer basket and bake for 14 minutes, flipping the patties halfway through, or until lightly browned and cooked through. 6. Meanwhile, melt the butter in a pan over medium heat. 7. Pour in the beer and whisk constantly, or until it begins to bubble. 8. Add the grated Colby cheese and mix well. Continue cooking for 3 to 4 minutes, or until the cheese melts. Remove the patties from the basket to a plate. Drizzle them with the cheese sauce and serve immediately.

Trout Amandine with Lemon Butter Sauce

Prep time: 20 minutes | Cook time: 8 minutes | Serves 4

Trout Amandine:	Lemon Butter Sauce:
80 g toasted almonds	8 tablespoons butter, melted
40 g grated Parmesan cheese	2 tablespoons freshly squeezed
1 teaspoon salt	lemon juice
½ teaspoon freshly ground black pepper	½ teaspoon Worcestershire sauce
2 tablespoons butter, melted	½ teaspoon salt
4 (115 g) trout fillets, or salmon fillets	½ teaspoon freshly ground black pepper
Cooking spray	¼ teaspoon hot sauce

1. In a blender or food processor, pulse the almonds for 5 to 10 seconds until finely processed. Transfer to a shallow bowl and whisk in the Parmesan cheese, salt, and pepper. Place the melted butter in another shallow bowl. 2. One at a time, dip the fish in the melted butter, then the almond mixture, coating thoroughly. 3. Preheat the air fryer to 148°C. Line the air fryer basket with baking paper. 4. Place the coated fish on the baking paper and spritz with oil. 5. Bake for 4 minutes. Flip the fish, spritz it with oil, and bake for 4 minutes more until the fish flakes easily with a fork. 6. In a small bowl, whisk the butter, lemon juice, Worcestershire sauce, salt, pepper, and hot sauce until blended. 7. Serve with the fish.

Air Fryer Fish Fry

Prep time: 5 minutes | Cook time: 15 minutes | Serves 4

500 ml low-fat buttermilk
½ teaspoon garlic powder
½ teaspoon onion powder
4 (115 g) flounder fillets

60 g plain yellow cornmeal
60 g chickpea flour
¼ teaspoon cayenne pepper
Freshly ground black pepper

1. In a large bowl, combine the buttermilk, garlic powder, and onion powder. 2. Add the flounder, turning until well coated, and set aside to marinate for 20 minutes. 3. In a shallow bowl, stir the cornmeal, chickpea flour, cayenne, and pepper together. 4. Dredge the fillets in the meal mixture, turning until well coated. Place in the basket of an air fryer. 5. Set the air fryer to 193°C, close, and cook for 12 minutes.

Chapter 6 Beef, Pork, and Lamb

Lemony Pork Loin Chop Schnitzel

**Prep time: 15 minutes | Cook time: 15 minutes |
Serves 4**

4 thin boneless pork loin chops
2 tablespoons lemon juice
60 g flour
¼ teaspoon marjoram
1 teaspoon salt

125 g panko breadcrumbs
2 eggs
Lemon wedges, for serving
Cooking spray

1. Preheat the air fryer to 200°C and spritz with cooking spray. 2.
On a clean work surface, drizzle the pork chops with lemon juice
on both sides. 3. Combine the flour with marjoram and salt on a
shallow plate. Pour the breadcrumbs on a separate shallow dish.
Beat the eggs in a large bowl. 4. Dredge the pork chops in the flour,
then dunk in the beaten eggs to coat well. Shake the excess off and
roll over the breadcrumbs. 5. Arrange the chops in the preheated
air fryer and spritz with cooking spray. Air fry for 15 minutes
or until the chops are golden and crispy. Flip the chops halfway
through. Squeeze the lemon wedges over the fried chops and serve
immediately.

Spinach and Edam Steak Rolls

**Prep time: 10 minutes | Cook time: 12 minutes |
Makes 8 rolls**

1 (450 g) flank steak, butterflied
8 (30 g, ¼-inch-thick) deli slices
Edam cheese

20 g fresh spinach leaves
½ teaspoon salt
¼ teaspoon ground black pepper

1. Place steak on a large plate. Place Edam slices to cover steak,
leaving 1-inch at the edges. Lay spinach leaves over cheese. Gently
roll steak and tie with kitchen twine or secure with toothpicks.
Carefully slice into eight pieces. Sprinkle each with salt and pepper.
2. Place rolls into ungreased air fryer basket, cut side up. Adjust the
temperature to 204°C and air fry for 12 minutes. Steak rolls will be
browned and cheese will be melted when done and have an internal
temperature of at least 64°C for medium steak and 82°C for well-
done steak. Serve warm.

Mongolian-Style Beef

**Prep time: 10 minutes | Cook time: 10 minutes |
Serves 4**

Oil, for spraying
30 g cornflour
450 g flank steak, thinly sliced
95 g Packed light brown sugar
125 g soy sauce
2 teaspoons toasted sesame oil

1 tablespoon minced garlic
½ teaspoon ground ginger
125 ml water
Cooked white rice or ramen
noodles, for serving

1. Line the air fryer basket with baking paper and spray lightly

with oil. 2. Place the cornflour in a bowl and dredge the steak
until evenly coated. Shake off any excess cornflour. 3. Place the
steak in the prepared basket and spray lightly with oil. 4. Roast at
200°C for 5 minutes, flip, and cook for another 5 minutes. 5. In a
small saucepan, combine the brown sugar, soy sauce, sesame oil,
garlic, ginger, and water and bring to a boil over medium-high heat,
stirring frequently. Remove from the heat. 6. Transfer the meat to
the sauce and toss until evenly coated. Let sit for about 5 minutes
so the steak absorbs the flavors. Serve with white rice or ramen
noodles.

Beef and Tomato Sauce Meatloaf

**Prep time: 15 minutes | Cook time: 25 minutes |
Serves 4**

680 g minced beef
250 g tomato sauce
60 g breadcrumbs
2 egg whites
60 g grated Parmesan cheese
1 diced onion
2 tablespoons chopped parsley

2 tablespoons minced ginger
2 garlic cloves, minced
½ teaspoon dried basil
1 teaspoon cayenne pepper
Salt and ground black pepper, to
taste
Cooking spray

1. Preheat the air fryer to 180°C. Spritz a meatloaf pan with
cooking spray. 2. Combine all the ingredients in a large bowl. Stir
to mix well. 3. Pour the meat mixture in the prepared meatloaf pan
and press with a spatula to make it firm. 4. Arrange the pan in the
preheated air fryer and bake for 25 minutes or until the beef is well
browned. 5. Serve immediately.

Sichuan Cumin Lamb

**Prep time: 30 minutes | Cook time: 10 minutes |
Serves 4**

Lamb:
2 tablespoons cumin seeds
1 teaspoon Sichuan peppercorns,
or ½ teaspoon cayenne pepper
450 g lamb (preferably
shoulder), cut into ½ by 2-inch
pieces
2 tablespoons vegetable oil
1 tablespoon light soy sauce

1 tablespoon minced garlic
2 fresh red chillies, chopped
1 teaspoon kosher or coarse sea
salt
¼ teaspoon sugar
For Serving:
2 spring onions, chopped
Large handful of chopped fresh
coriander

1. For the lamb: In a dry skillet, toast the cumin seeds and Sichuan
peppercorns (if using) over medium heat, stirring frequently, until
fragrant, 1 to 2 minutes. Remove from the heat and let cool. Use
a mortar and pestle to coarsely grind the toasted spices. 2. Use a
fork to pierce the lamb pieces to allow the marinade to penetrate
better. In a large bowl or sandwich bag, combine the toasted spices,
vegetable oil, soy sauce, garlic, chillies, salt, and sugar. Add the
lamb to the bag. Seal and massage to coat. Marinate at room
temperature for 30 minutes. 3. Place the lamb in a single layer in
the air fryer basket. Set the air fryer to 176°C for 10 minutes. Use

a meat thermometer to ensure the lamb has reached an internal temperature of 64°C (medium-rare). 4. Transfer the lamb to a serving bowl. Stir in the spring onions and coriander and serve.

Sausage and Peppers

Prep time: 7 minutes | Cook time: 35 minutes | Serves 4

Oil, for spraying	1 tablespoon olive oil
910 g spicy or sweet Italian sausage links, cut into thick slices	1 tablespoon chopped fresh parsley
4 large bell peppers of any color, seeded and cut into slices	1 teaspoon dried oregano
	1 teaspoon dried basil
1 onion, thinly sliced	1 teaspoon balsamic vinegar

1. Line the air fryer basket with baking paper and spray lightly with oil. 2. In a large bowl, combine the sausage, bell peppers, and onion. 3. In a small bowl, whisk together the olive oil, parsley, oregano, basil, and balsamic vinegar. Pour the mixture over the sausage and peppers and toss until evenly coated. 4. Using a slotted spoon, transfer the mixture to the prepared basket, taking care to drain out as much excess liquid as possible. 5. Air fry at 176°C for 20 minutes, stir, and cook for another 15 minutes, or until the sausage is browned and the juices run clear.

Bacon-Wrapped Pork Tenderloin

Prep time: 30 minutes | Cook time: 22 to 25 minutes | Serves 6

60 g minced onion	¼ teaspoon freshly ground black pepper
125 ml hard apple cider, or apple juice	
60 g honey	910 g pork tenderloin
1 tablespoon minced garlic	1 to 2 tablespoons oil
¼ teaspoon salt	8 uncooked bacon slices

1. In a medium bowl, stir together the onion, hard cider, honey, garlic, salt, and pepper. Transfer to a large sandwich bag or airtight container and add the pork. Seal the bag. Refrigerate to marinate for at least 2 hours. 2. Preheat the air fryer to 204°C. Line the air fryer basket with baking paper. 3. Remove the pork from the marinade and place it on the baking paper. Spritz with oil. 4. Cook for 15 minutes. 5. Wrap the bacon slices around the pork and secure them with toothpicks. Turn the pork roast and spritz with oil. Cook for 7 to 10 minutes more until the internal temperature reaches 64°C, depending on how well-done you like pork loin. It will continue cooking after it's removed from the fryer, so let it sit for 5 minutes before serving.

Marinated Steak Tips with Mushrooms

Prep time: 30 minutes | Cook time: 10 minutes | Serves 4

680 g sirloin, trimmed and cut into 1-inch pieces	60 g Worcestershire sauce
230 g brown mushrooms, halved	1 tablespoon Dijon mustard
	1 tablespoon olive oil
	1 teaspoon paprika

1 teaspoon crushed red pepper flakes	2 tablespoons chopped fresh parsley (optional)

1. Place the beef and mushrooms in an extra-large freezer bag. In a small bowl, whisk together the Worcestershire, mustard, olive oil, paprika, and red pepper flakes. Pour the marinade into the bag and massage gently to ensure the beef and mushrooms are evenly coated. Seal the bag and refrigerate for at least 4 hours, preferably overnight. Remove from the refrigerator 30 minutes before cooking. 2. Preheat the air fryer to 204°C. 3. Drain and discard the marinade. Arrange the steak and mushrooms in the air fryer basket. Air fry for 10 minutes, pausing halfway through the baking time to shake the basket. Transfer to a serving plate and top with the parsley, if desired.

Pork Loin Roast

Prep time: 30 minutes | Cook time: 55 minutes | Serves 6

680 g boneless pork loin roast, washed	¾ teaspoon sea salt flakes
1 teaspoon mustard seeds	1 teaspoon red pepper flakes, crushed
1 teaspoon garlic powder	2 dried sprigs thyme, crushed
1 teaspoon porcini powder	2 tablespoons lime juice
1 teaspoon shallot powder	

1. Firstly, score the meat using a small knife; make sure to not cut too deep. 2. In a small-sized mixing dish, combine all seasonings in the order listed above; mix to combine well. 3. Massage the spice mix into the pork meat to evenly distribute. Drizzle with lemon juice. 4. Set the air fryer to 180°C. Place the pork in the air fryer basket; roast for 25 to 30 minutes. Pause the machine, check for doneness and cook for 25 minutes more.

Parmesan-Crusted Pork Chops

Prep time: 5 minutes | Cook time: 12 minutes | Serves 4

1 large egg	½ teaspoon salt
60 g grated Parmesan cheese	¼ teaspoon ground black pepper
4 (115 g) boneless pork chops	

1. Whisk egg in a medium bowl and place Parmesan in a separate medium bowl. 2. Sprinkle pork chops on both sides with salt and pepper. Dip each pork chop into egg, then press both sides into Parmesan. 3. Place pork chops into ungreased air fryer basket. Adjust the temperature to 204°C and air fry for 12 minutes, turning chops halfway through cooking. Pork chops will be golden and have an internal temperature of at least 64°C when done. Serve warm.

Bulgogi Burgers

Prep time: 30 minutes | Cook time: 10 minutes | Serves 4

Burgers:	2 tablespoons gochujang
450 g 85% lean ground beef	(Korean red chilli paste)
30 g chopped spring onions	1 tablespoon dark soy sauce

2 teaspoons minced garlic	60 g mayonnaise
2 teaspoons minced fresh ginger	30 g chopped spring onions
2 teaspoons sugar	1 tablespoon gochujang (Korean
1 tablespoon toasted sesame oil	red chilli paste)
½ teaspoon kosher or coarse sea	1 tablespoon toasted sesame oil
salt	2 teaspoons sesame seeds
Gochujang Mayonnaise:	4 hamburger buns

1. For the burgers: In a large bowl, mix the ground beef, spring onions, gochujang, soy sauce, garlic, ginger, sugar, sesame oil, and salt. Marinate at room temperature for 30 minutes, or cover and refrigerate for up to 24 hours. 2. Divide the meat into four portions and form them into round patties. Make a slight depression in the middle of each patty with your thumb to prevent them from puffing up into a dome shape while cooking. 3. Place the patties in a single layer in the air fryer basket. Set the air fryer to 176ºC for 10 minutes. 4. Meanwhile, for the gochujang mayonnaise: Stir together the mayonnaise, spring onions, gochujang, sesame oil, and sesame seeds. 5. At the end of the cooking time, use a meat thermometer to ensure the burgers have reached an internal temperature of 72ºC (medium). 6. To serve, place the burgers on the buns and top with the mayonnaise.

Teriyaki Rump Steak with Broccoli and Capsicum

Prep time: 5 minutes | Cook time: 13 minutes | Serves 4

230 grump steak	2 red capsicums, sliced
85 ml teriyaki marinade	Fine sea salt and ground black
1½ teaspoons sesame oil	pepper, to taste
½ head broccoli, cut into florets	Cooking spray

1. Toss the rump steak in a large bowl with teriyaki marinade. Wrap the bowl in plastic and refrigerate to marinate for at least an hour. 2. Preheat the air fryer to 204ºC and spritz with cooking spray. 3. Discard the marinade and transfer the steak in the preheated air fryer. Spritz with cooking spray. 4. Air fry for 13 minutes or until well browned. Flip the steak halfway through. 5. Meanwhile, heat the sesame oil in a nonstick skillet over medium heat. Add the broccoli and capsicum. Sprinkle with salt and ground black pepper. Sauté for 5 minutes or until the broccoli is tender. 6. Transfer the air fried rump steak on a plate and top with the sautéed broccoli and capsicum. Serve hot.

Indian Minted Lamb Kebabs

Prep time: 30 minutes | Cook time: 15 minutes | Serves 4

450 g ground lamb	½ teaspoon cayenne pepper
60 g finely minced onion	¼ teaspoon ground cardamom
5 g chopped fresh mint	¼ teaspoon ground cinnamon
5 g chopped fresh coriander	1 teaspoon kosher or coarse sea
1 tablespoon minced garlic	salt
½ teaspoon ground turmeric	

1. In the bowl of a stand mixer fitted with the paddle attachment, combine the lamb, onion, mint, coriander, garlic, turmeric, cayenne, cardamom, cinnamon, and salt. Mix on low speed until you have a

sticky mess of spiced meat. If you have time, let the mixture stand at room temperature for 30 minutes (or cover and refrigerate for up to a day or two, until you're ready to make the kebabs). 2. Divide the meat into eight equal portions. Form each into a long sausage shape. Place the kebabs in a single layer in the air fryer basket. Set the air fryer to 176ºC for 10 minutes. Increase the air fryer temperature to 204ºC and cook for 3 to 4 minutes more to brown the kebabs. Use a meat thermometer to ensure the kebabs have reached an internal temperature of 72ºC (medium).

Greek Pork with Tzatziki Sauce

Prep time: 30 minutes | Cook time: 50 minutes | Serves 4

Greek Pork:	2 cloves garlic, finely chopped
910 g pork sirloin roast	Tzatziki:
Salt and black pepper, to taste	½ cucumber, finely chopped and
1 teaspoon smoked paprika	squeezed
½ teaspoon mustard seeds	250 ml full-fat Greek yogurt
½ teaspoon celery seeds	1 garlic clove, minced
1 teaspoon fennel seeds	1 tablespoon extra-virgin olive
1 teaspoon Ancho chilli powder	oil
1 teaspoon turmeric powder	1 teaspoon balsamic vinegar
½ teaspoon ground ginger	1 teaspoon minced fresh dill
2 tablespoons olive oil	A pinch of salt

1. Toss all ingredients for Greek pork in a large mixing bowl. Toss until the meat is well coated. 2. Cook in the preheated air fryer at 180ºC for 30 minutes; turn over and cook another 20 minutes. 3. Meanwhile, prepare the tzatziki by mixing all the tzatziki ingredients. Place in your refrigerator until ready to use. 4. Serve the pork sirloin roast with the chilled tzatziki on the side. Enjoy!

Spicy Lamb Sirloin Chops

Prep time: 30 minutes | Cook time: 15 minutes | Serves 4

½ yellow onion, coarsely	1 teaspoon ground cinnamon
chopped	1 teaspoon ground turmeric
4 coin-sized slices peeled fresh	½ to 1 teaspoon cayenne pepper
ginger	½ teaspoon ground cardamom
5 garlic cloves	1 teaspoon kosher or coarse sea
1 teaspoon garam masala	salt
1 teaspoon ground fennel	450 g lamb sirloin chops

1. In a blender, combine the onion, ginger, garlic, garam masala, fennel, cinnamon, turmeric, cayenne, cardamom, and salt. Pulse until the onion is finely minced and the mixture forms a thick paste, 3 to 4 minutes. 2. Place the lamb chops in a large bowl. Slash the meat and fat with a sharp knife several times to allow the marinade to penetrate better. Add the spice paste to the bowl and toss the lamb to coat. Marinate at room temperature for 30 minutes or cover and refrigerate for up to 24 hours. 3. Place the lamb chops in a single layer in the air fryer basket. Set the air fryer to 164ºC for 15 minutes, turning the chops halfway through the cooking time. Use a meat thermometer to ensure the lamb has reached an internal temperature of 64ºC (medium-rare).

Mexican Pork Chops

¼ teaspoon dried oregano	2 (115 g) boneless pork chops
1½ teaspoons taco seasoning mix	2 tablespoons unsalted butter, divided

1. Preheat the air fryer to 204°C. 2. Combine the dried oregano and taco seasoning in a small bowl and rub the mixture into the pork chops. Brush the chops with 1 tablespoon butter. 3. In the air fryer, air fry the chops for 15 minutes, turning them over halfway through to air fry on the other side. 4. When the chops are a brown color, check the internal temperature has reached 64°C and remove from the air fryer. Serve with a garnish of remaining butter.

Cantonese BBQ Pork

60 g honey	2 teaspoons minced garlic
2 tablespoons dark soy sauce	2 teaspoons minced fresh ginger
1 tablespoon sugar	1 teaspoon Chinese five-spice powder
1 tablespoon Shaoxing wine (rice cooking wine)	
1 tablespoon hoisin sauce	450 g fatty pork shoulder, cut into long, 1-inch-thick pieces

1. In a small microwave-safe bowl, combine the honey, soy sauce, sugar, wine, hoisin, garlic, ginger, and five-spice powder. Microwave in 10-second intervals, stirring in between, until the honey has dissolved. 2. Use a fork to pierce the pork slices to allow the marinade to penetrate better. Place the pork in a large bowl or large sandwich bag and pour in half the marinade; set aside the remaining marinade to use for the sauce. Toss to coat. Marinate the pork at room temperature for 30 minutes, or cover and refrigerate for up 24 hours. 3. Place the pork in a single layer in the air fryer basket. Set the air fryer to 204°C for 15 minutes, turning and basting the pork halfway through the cooking time. 4. While the pork is cooking, microwave the reserved marinade on high for 45 to 60 seconds, stirring every 15 seconds, to thicken it slightly to the consistency of a sauce. 5. Transfer the pork to a cutting board and let rest for 10 minutes. Brush with the sauce and serve.
Reuben Beef Rolls with Thousand Island Sauce
Prep time: 15 minutes | Cook time: 10 minutes per batch | Makes 10 rolls

230 g cooked corned beef, chopped

60 g drained and chopped sauerkraut

1 (230 g) package cream cheese, softened	60 g tomato sauce
	190 g mayonnaise
60 g shredded Swiss cheese	Fresh thyme leaves, for garnish
20 slices prosciutto	
Cooking spray	2 tablespoons sugar
Thousand Island Sauce:	⅛ teaspoon fine sea salt
30 g chopped dill pickles	Ground black pepper, to taste

1. Preheat the air fryer to 204°C and spritz with cooking spray. 2. Combine the beef, sauerkraut, cream cheese, and Swiss cheese in a large bowl. Stir to mix well. 3. Unroll a slice of prosciutto on a clean work surface, then top with another slice of prosciutto crosswise. Scoop up 4 tablespoons of the beef mixture in the center. 4. Fold the top slice sides over the filling as the ends of the roll, then roll up the long sides of the bottom prosciutto and make it into a roll shape. Overlap the sides by about 1 inch. Repeat with remaining filling and prosciutto. 5. Arrange the rolls in the preheated air fryer, seam side down, and spritz with cooking spray. 6. Air fry for 10 minutes or until golden and crispy. Flip the rolls halfway through. Work in batches to avoid overcrowding. 7. Meanwhile, combine the ingredients for the sauce in a small bowl. Stir to mix well. 8. Serve the rolls with the dipping sauce.

Pork Cutlets with Aloha Salsa

Aloha Salsa:	2 eggs
125 g fresh pineapple, chopped in small pieces	2 tablespoons milk
	30 g plain flour
30 g red onion, finely chopped	30 g panko bread crumbs
30 g green or red bell pepper, chopped	4 teaspoons sesame seeds
	450 g boneless, thin pork cutlets
½ teaspoon ground cinnamon	(⅜- to ½-inch thick)
1 teaspoon low-sodium soy sauce	Lemon pepper and salt
	30 g cornflour
⅛ teaspoon crushed red pepper	Oil for misting or cooking spray
⅛ teaspoon ground black pepper	

1. In a medium bowl, stir together all ingredients for salsa. Cover and refrigerate while cooking pork. 2. Preheat the air fryer to 200°C. 3. Beat together eggs and milk in shallow dish. 4. In another shallow dish, mix together the flour, panko, and sesame seeds. 5. Sprinkle pork cutlets with lemon pepper and salt to taste. Most lemon pepper seasoning contains salt, so go easy adding extra. 6. Dip pork cutlets in cornflour, egg mixture, and then panko coating. Spray both sides with oil or cooking spray. 7. Cook cutlets for 3 minutes. Turn cutlets over, spraying both sides, and continue cooking for 4 to 6 minutes or until well done. 8. Serve fried cutlets with salsa on the side.

Ground Beef Taco Rolls

230 g 20% minced beef	2 tablespoons chopped coriander
85 ml water	185 g shredded Mozzarella cheese
1 tablespoon chilli powder	
2 teaspoons cumin	60 g blanched finely ground almond flour
½ teaspoon garlic powder	
¼ teaspoon dried oregano	60 g full-fat cream cheese
30 g canned diced tomatoes and chillies, drained	1 large egg

1. In a medium skillet over medium heat, brown the minced beef about 7 to 10 minutes. When meat is fully cooked, drain. 2. Add water to skillet and stir in chilli powder, cumin, garlic powder, oregano, and tomatoes with chillies. Add coriander. Bring to a boil, then reduce heat to simmer for 3 minutes. 3. In a large microwave-safe bowl, place Mozzarella, almond flour, cream cheese, and egg. Microwave for 1 minute. Stir the mixture quickly until smooth

ball of dough forms. 4. Cut a piece of baking paper for your work surface. Press the dough into a large rectangle on the baking paper, wetting your hands to prevent the dough from sticking as necessary. Cut the dough into eight rectangles. 5. On each rectangle place a few spoons of the meat mixture. Fold the short ends of each roll toward the center and roll the length as you would a burrito. 6. Cut a piece of baking paper to fit your air fryer basket. Place taco rolls onto the baking paper and place into the air fryer basket. 7. Adjust the temperature to 180°C and air fry for 10 minutes. 8. Flip halfway through the cooking time. 9. Allow to cool 10 minutes before serving.

Vietnamese "Shaking" Beef

Prep time: 30 minutes | Cook time: 4 minutes per batch | Serves 4

Meat:
4 garlic cloves, minced
2 teaspoons soy sauce
2 teaspoons sugar
1 teaspoon toasted sesame oil
1 teaspoon kosher or coarse sea salt
¼ teaspoon black pepper
680 g flat iron or top sirloin steak, cut into 1-inch cubes
Salad:
2 tablespoons rice vinegar or apple cider vinegar
2 tablespoons vegetable oil
1 garlic clove, minced

2 teaspoons sugar
¼ teaspoon kosher or coarse sea salt
¼ teaspoon black pepper
½ red onion, halved and very thinly sliced
1 head lettuce, leaves separated and torn into large pieces
60 g halved grape tomatoes
5 g fresh mint leaves
For Serving:
Lime wedges
Coarse salt and freshly cracked black pepper, to taste

1. For the meat: In a small bowl, combine the garlic, soy sauce, sugar, sesame oil, salt, and pepper. Place the meat in an extra-large freezer bag. Pour the marinade over the meat. Seal and place the bag in a large bowl. Marinate for 30 minutes, or cover and refrigerate for up to 24 hours. 2. Place half the meat in the air fryer basket. Set the air fryer to 232°C for 4 minutes, shaking the basket to redistribute the meat halfway through the cooking time. Transfer the meat to a plate (it should be medium-rare, still pink in the middle). Cover lightly with aluminum foil. Repeat to cook the remaining meat. 3. Meanwhile, for the salad: In a large bowl, whisk together the vinegar, vegetable oil, garlic, sugar, salt, and pepper. Add the onion. Stir to combine. Add the lettuce, tomatoes, and mint and toss to combine. Arrange the salad on a serving platter. 4. Arrange the cooked meat over the salad. Drizzle any accumulated juices from the plate over the meat. Serve with lime wedges, coarse salt, and cracked black pepper.

Mojito Lamb Chops

Prep time: 30 minutes | Cook time: 5 minutes | Serves 2

Marinade:
2 teaspoons grated lime zest
125 ml lime juice
60 ml avocado oil
5 g chopped fresh mint leaves
4 cloves garlic, roughly chopped
2 teaspoons fine sea salt

½ teaspoon ground black pepper
4 (1-inch-thick) lamb chops
Sprigs of fresh mint, for garnish (optional)
Lime slices, for serving (optional)

1. Make the marinade: Place all the ingredients for the marinade in a food processor or blender and purée until mostly smooth with a few small chunks. Transfer half of the marinade to a shallow dish and set the other half aside for serving. Add the lamb to the shallow dish, cover, and place in the refrigerator to marinate for at least 2 hours or overnight. 2. Spray the air fryer basket with avocado oil. Preheat the air fryer to 200°C. 3. Remove the chops from the marinade and place them in the air fryer basket. Air fry for 5 minutes, or until the internal temperature reaches 64°C for medium doneness. 4. Allow the chops to rest for 10 minutes before serving with the rest of the marinade as a sauce. Garnish with fresh mint leaves and serve with lime slices, if desired. Best served fresh.

Mustard Herb Pork Tenderloin

Prep time: 5 minutes | Cook time: 20 minutes | Serves 6

60 g mayonnaise
2 tablespoons Dijon mustard
½ teaspoon dried thyme
¼ teaspoon dried rosemary

1 (450 g) pork tenderloin
½ teaspoon salt
¼ teaspoon ground black pepper

1. In a small bowl, mix mayonnaise, mustard, thyme, and rosemary. Brush tenderloin with mixture on all sides, then sprinkle with salt and pepper on all sides. 2. Place tenderloin into ungreased air fryer basket. Adjust the temperature to 204°C and air fry for 20 minutes, turning tenderloin halfway through cooking. Tenderloin will be golden and have an internal temperature of at least 64°C when done. Serve warm.

Red Curry Flank Steak

Prep time: 30 minutes | Cook time: 12 to 18 minutes | Serves 4

3 tablespoons red curry paste
60 ml olive oil
2 teaspoons grated fresh ginger
2 tablespoons soy sauce
2 tablespoons rice wine vinegar

3 spring onions, minced
680 g flank steak
Fresh coriander (or parsley) leaves

1. Mix the red curry paste, olive oil, ginger, soy sauce, rice vinegar and spring onions together in a bowl. Place the flank steak in a shallow glass dish and pour half the marinade over the steak. Pierce the steak several times with a fork or meat tenderizer to let the marinade penetrate the meat. Turn the steak over, pour the remaining marinade over the top and pierce the steak several times again. Cover and marinate the steak in the refrigerator for 6 to 8 hours. 2. When you are ready to cook, remove the steak from the refrigerator and let it sit at room temperature for 30 minutes. 3. Preheat the air fryer to 204°C. 4. Cut the flank steak in half so that it fits more easily into the air fryer and transfer both pieces to the air fryer basket. Pour the marinade over the steak. Air fry for 12 to 18 minutes, depending on your preferred degree of doneness of the steak (12 minutes = medium rare). Flip the steak over halfway through the cooking time. 5. When your desired degree of doneness has been reached, remove the steak to a cutting board and let it rest for 5 minutes before slicing. Thinly slice the flank steak against the grain of the meat. Transfer the slices to a serving platter, pour any juice from the bottom of the air fryer over the sliced flank steak and

sprinkle the fresh coriander on top.

Five-Spice Pork Belly

Prep time: 10 minutes | Cook time: 17 minutes | Serves 4

450 g unsalted pork belly
2 teaspoons Chinese five-spice powder
Sauce:
1 tablespoon coconut oil
1 (1-inch) piece fresh ginger, peeled and grated
2 cloves garlic, minced

125 ml beef or chicken stock
50 g powdered sweetener or equivalent amount of liquid sweetener
3 tablespoons wheat-free tamari, or 125 g coconut aminos
1 spring onion, sliced, plus more for garnish

1. Spray the air fryer basket with avocado oil. Preheat the air fryer to 204ºC. 2. Cut the pork belly into ½-inch-thick slices and season well on all sides with the five-spice powder. Place the slices in a single layer in the air fryer basket (if you're using a smaller air fryer, work in batches if necessary) and cook for 8 minutes, or until cooked to your liking, flipping halfway through. 3. While the pork belly cooks, make the sauce: Heat the coconut oil in a small saucepan over medium heat. Add the ginger and garlic and sauté for 1 minute, or until fragrant. Add the stock, sweetener, and tamari and simmer for 10 to 15 minutes, until thickened. Add the spring onion and cook for another minute, until the spring onion is softened. Taste and adjust the seasoning to your liking. 4. Transfer the pork belly to a large bowl. Pour the sauce over the pork belly and coat well. Place the pork belly slices on a serving platter and garnish with sliced spring onions. 5. Best served fresh. Store leftovers in an airtight container in the fridge for up to 4 days. Reheat in a preheated 204ºC air fryer for 3 minutes, or until heated through.

Greek-Style Meatloaf

Prep time: 5 minutes | Cook time: 25 minutes | Serves 6

450 g lean minced beef
2 eggs
2 plum tomatoes, diced
½ white onion, diced
60 g whole wheat bread crumbs
1 teaspoon garlic powder
1 teaspoon dried oregano
1 teaspoon dried thyme

1 teaspoon salt
1 teaspoon black pepper
60 g mozzarella cheese, shredded
1 tablespoon olive oil
Fresh chopped parsley, for garnish

1. Preheat the oven to 192ºC. 2. In a large bowl, mix together the minced beef, eggs, tomatoes, onion, bread crumbs, garlic powder, oregano, thyme, salt, pepper, and cheese. 3. Form into a loaf, flattening to 1-inch thick. 4. Brush the top with olive oil, then place the meatloaf into the air fryer basket and cook for 25 minutes. 5. Remove from the air fryer and allow to rest for 5 minutes, before slicing and serving with a sprinkle of parsley.

Herb-Crusted Lamb Chops

Prep time: 10 minutes | Cook time: 5 minutes | Serves 2

1 large egg
2 cloves garlic, minced
30 g pork scratchings, ground to dust
30 g powdered Parmesan cheese
1 tablespoon chopped fresh oregano leaves
1 tablespoon chopped fresh rosemary leaves
1 teaspoon chopped fresh thyme

leaves
½ teaspoon ground black pepper
4 (1-inch-thick) lamb chops
For Garnish/Serving (Optional):
Sprigs of fresh oregano
Sprigs of fresh rosemary
Sprigs of fresh thyme
Lavender flowers
Lemon slices

1. Spray the air fryer basket with avocado oil. Preheat the air fryer to 204ºC. 2. Beat the egg in a shallow bowl, add the garlic, and stir well to combine. In another shallow bowl, mix together the pork dust, Parmesan, herbs, and pepper. 3. One at a time, dip the lamb chops into the egg mixture, shake off the excess egg, and then dredge them in the Parmesan mixture. Use your hands to coat the chops well in the Parmesan mixture and form a nice crust on all sides; if necessary, dip the chops again in both the egg and the Parmesan mixture. 4. Place the lamb chops in the air fryer basket, leaving space between them, and air fry for 5 minutes, or until the internal temperature reaches 64ºC for medium doneness. Allow to rest for 10 minutes before serving. 5. Garnish with sprigs of oregano, rosemary, and thyme, and lavender flowers, if desired. Serve with lemon slices, if desired. 6. Best served fresh. Store leftovers in an airtight container in the fridge for up to 4 days. Serve chilled over a salad, or reheat in a 176ºC air fryer for 3 minutes, or until heated through.

Spaghetti Zoodles and Meatballs

Prep time: 30 minutes | Cook time: 11 to 13 minutes | Serves 6

450 g minced beef
1½ teaspoons sea salt, plus more for seasoning
1 large egg, beaten
1 teaspoon gelatin
95 g Parmesan cheese
2 teaspoons minced garlic
1 teaspoon Italian seasoning

Freshly ground black pepper, to taste
Avocado oil spray
Keto-friendly marinara sauce, for serving
170 g courgette noodles, made using a spiraliser or store-bought

1. Place the minced beef in a large bowl, and season with the salt. 2. Place the egg in a separate bowl and sprinkle with the gelatin. Allow to sit for 5 minutes. 3. Stir the gelatin mixture, then pour it over the minced beef. Add the Parmesan, garlic, and Italian seasoning. Season with salt and pepper. 4. Form the mixture into 1½-inch meatballs and place them on a plate; cover with plastic wrap and refrigerate for at least 1 hour or overnight. 5. Spray the meatballs with oil. Set the air fryer to 204ºC and arrange the meatballs in a single layer in the air fryer basket. Air fry for 4 minutes. Flip the meatballs and spray them with more oil. Air fry for 4 minutes more, until an instant-read thermometer reads 72ºC. Transfer the meatballs to a plate and allow them to rest. 6. While the meatballs are resting, heat the marinara in a saucepan on the stove over medium heat. 7. Place the courgette noodles in the air fryer, and cook at 204ºC for 3 to 5 minutes. 8. To serve, place the courgette noodles in serving bowls. Top with meatballs and warm marinara.

Chapter 7 Snacks and Appetisers

Chapter 7 Snacks and Appetisers

Crispy Mozzarella Sticks

Prep time: 8 minutes | Cook time: 5 minutes | Serves 4

60 g plain flour
1 egg, beaten
60 g panko bread crumbs
60 g grated Parmesan cheese
1 teaspoon Italian seasoning

½ teaspoon garlic salt
6 Mozzarella sticks, halved crosswise
Olive oil spray

1. Put the flour in a small bowl. 2. Put the beaten egg in another small bowl. 3. In a medium bowl, stir together the panko, Parmesan cheese, Italian seasoning, and garlic salt. 4. Roll a Mozzarella-stick half in the flour, dip it into the egg, and then roll it in the panko mixture to coat. Press the coating lightly to make sure the bread crumbs stick to the cheese. Repeat with the remaining 11 Mozzarella sticks. 5. Insert the crisper plate into the basket and the basket into the unit. Preheat the unit by selecting AIR FRY, setting the temperature to 204ºC, and setting the time to 3 minutes. Select START/STOP to begin. 6. Once the unit is preheated, spray the crisper plate with olive oil and place a baking paper liner in the basket. Place the Mozzarella sticks into the basket and lightly spray them with olive oil. 7. Select AIR FRY, set the temperature to 204ºC, and set the time to 5 minutes. Select START/STOP to begin. 8. When the cooking is complete, the Mozzarella sticks should be golden and crispy. Let the sticks stand for 1 minute before transferring them to a serving plate. Serve warm.

Sweet Potato Fries with Mayonnaise

Prep time: 5 minutes | Cook time: 20 minutes | Serves 2 to 3

1 large sweet potato (about 450 g), scrubbed
1 teaspoon vegetable or canola oil
Salt, to taste
Dipping Sauce:

60 g light mayonnaise
½ teaspoon Sriracha sauce
1 tablespoon spicy brown mustard
1 tablespoon Thai sweet chilli sauce

1. Preheat the air fryer to 92ºC. 2. On a flat work surface, cut the sweet potato into fry-shaped strips about ¼ inch wide and ¼ inch thick. You can use a mandoline to slice the sweet potato quickly and uniformly. 3. In a medium bowl, drizzle the sweet potato strips with the oil and toss well. 4. Transfer to the air fryer basket and air fry for 10 minutes, shaking the basket twice during cooking. 5. Remove the air fryer basket and sprinkle with the salt and toss to coat. 6. Increase the air fryer temperature to 204ºC and air fry for an additional 10 minutes, or until the fries are crispy and tender. Shake the basket a few times during cooking. 7. Meanwhile, whisk together all the ingredients for the sauce in a small bowl. 8. Remove the sweet potato fries from the basket to a plate and serve warm alongside the dipping sauce.

Greek Potato Skins with Olives and Feta

Prep time: 5 minutes | Cook time: 45 minutes | Serves 4

2 russet potatoes
3 tablespoons olive oil, divided, plus more for drizzling (optional)
1 teaspoon kosher or coarse sea salt, divided
¼ teaspoon black pepper

2 tablespoons fresh coriander, chopped, plus more for serving
30 g Kalamata olives, diced
30 g crumbled feta
Chopped fresh parsley, for garnish (optional)

1. Preheat the air fryer to 192ºC. 2. Using a fork, poke 2 to 3 holes in the potatoes, then coat each with about ½ tablespoon olive oil and ½ teaspoon salt. 3. Place the potatoes into the air fryer basket and bake for 30 minutes. 4. Remove the potatoes from the air fryer, and slice in half. Using a spoon, scoop out the flesh of the potatoes, leaving a ½-inch layer of potato inside the skins, and set the skins aside. 5. In a medium bowl, combine the scooped potato middles with the remaining 2 tablespoons of olive oil, ½ teaspoon of salt, black pepper, and coriander. Mix until well combined. 6. Divide the potato filling into the now-empty potato skins, spreading it evenly over them. Top each potato with a tablespoon each of the olives and feta. 7. Place the loaded potato skins back into the air fryer and bake for 15 minutes. 8. Serve with additional chopped coriander or parsley and a drizzle of olive oil, if desired.

Lemon Prawns with Garlic Olive Oil

Prep time: 5 minutes | Cook time: 6 minutes | Serves 4

450 g medium prawns, cleaned and deveined
90 ml olive oil, divided
Juice of ½ lemon
3 garlic cloves, minced and divided

½ teaspoon salt
¼ teaspoon red pepper flakes
Lemon wedges, for serving (optional)
Marinara sauce, for dipping (optional)

1. Preheat the air fryer to 192ºC. 2. In a large bowl, combine the prawns with 2 tablespoons of the olive oil, as well as the lemon juice, half of the minced garlic, salt, and red pepper flakes. Toss to coat the prawns well. 3. In a small ramekin, combine the remaining 60 ml olive oil and the remaining minced garlic. 4. Tear off a 12-by-12-inch sheet of aluminum foil. Pour the prawns into the center of the foil, then fold the sides up and crimp the edges so that it forms an aluminum foil bowl that is open on top. Place this packet into the air fryer basket. 5. Roast the prawns for 4 minutes, then open the air fryer and place the ramekin with oil and garlic in the basket beside the prawn packet. Cook for 2 more minutes. 6. Transfer the prawns on to a serving plate or platter with the ramekin of garlic olive oil on the side for dipping. You may also serve with lemon wedges and marinara sauce, if desired.

String Bean Fries

Prep time: 15 minutes | Cook time: 5 to 6 minutes | Serves 4

230 g fresh string beans
2 eggs
4 teaspoons water
60 g plain flour
60 g bread crumbs

¼ teaspoon salt
¼ teaspoon ground black pepper
¼ teaspoon dry mustard (optional)
Oil for misting or cooking spray

1. Preheat the air fryer to 180ºC. 2. Trim stem ends from string beans, wash, and pat dry. 3. In a shallow dish, beat eggs and water together until well blended. 4. Place flour in a second shallow dish. 5. In a third shallow dish, stir together the bread crumbs, salt, pepper, and dry mustard if using. 6. Dip each string bean in egg mixture, flour, egg mixture again, then bread crumbs. 7. When you finish coating all the string beans, open air fryer and place them in basket. 8. Cook for 3 minutes. 9. Stop and mist string beans with oil or cooking spray. 10. Cook for 2 to 3 more minutes or until string beans are crispy and nicely browned.

Cinnamon Apple Chips

Prep time: 5 minutes | Cook time: 7 to 8 hours | Serves 4

4 medium apples, any type, cored and cut into ⅓-inch-thick slices (thin slices yield crunchy

chips)
¼ teaspoon ground cinnamon
¼ teaspoon ground nutmeg

1. Place the apple slices in a large bowl. Sprinkle the cinnamon and nutmeg onto the apple slices and toss to coat. 2. Insert the crisper plate into the basket and the basket into the unit. Preheat the unit by selecting DEHYDRATE, setting the temperature to 56ºC, and setting the time to 3 minutes. Select START/STOP to begin. 3. Once the unit is preheated, place the apple chips into the basket. It is okay to stack them. 4. Select DEHYDRATE, set the temperature to 56ºC, and set the time to 7 or 8 hours. Select START/STOP to begin. 5. When the cooking is complete, cool the apple chips. Serve or store at room temperature in an airtight container for up to 1 week.

Garlic-Parmesan Croutons

Prep time: 3 minutes | Cook time: 12 minutes | Serves 4

Oil, for spraying
500 g cubed French bread
1 tablespoon grated Parmesan cheese

3 tablespoons olive oil
1 tablespoon garlic granules
½ teaspoon unsalted salt

1. Line the air fryer basket with baking paper and spray lightly with oil. 2. In a large bowl, mix together the bread, Parmesan cheese, olive oil, garlic, and salt, tossing with your hands to evenly distribute the seasonings. Transfer the coated bread cubes to the prepared basket. 3. Air fry at 176ºC for 10 to 12 minutes, stirring once after 5 minutes, or until crisp and golden brown.

Cinnamon-Apple Chips

Prep time: 10 minutes | Cook time: 32 minutes | Serves 4

Oil, for spraying
2 Red Delicious or Honeycrisp apples

¼ teaspoon ground cinnamon, divided

1. Line the air fryer basket with baking paper and spray lightly with oil. 2. Trim the uneven ends off the apples. Using a mandoline on the thinnest setting or a sharp knife, cut the apples into very thin slices. Discard the cores. 3. Place half of the apple slices in a single layer in the prepared basket and sprinkle with half of the cinnamon. 4. Place a metal air fryer trivet on top of the apples to keep them from flying around while they are cooking. 5. Air fry at 148ºC for 16 minutes, flipping every 5 minutes to ensure even cooking. Repeat with the remaining apple slices and cinnamon. 6. Let cool to room temperature before serving. The chips will firm up as they cool.

Fried Artichoke Hearts

Prep time: 10 minutes | Cook time: 12 minutes | Serves 10

Oil, for spraying
3 (400 g) cans quartered artichokes, drained and patted dry
125 g mayonnaise

125 g panko bread crumbs
40 g grated Parmesan cheese
Salt and freshly ground black pepper, to taste

1. Line the air fryer basket with baking paper and spray lightly with oil. 2. Place the artichokes on a plate. Put the mayonnaise and bread crumbs in separate bowls. 3. Working one at a time, dredge each artichoke piece in the mayonnaise, then in the bread crumbs to cover. 4. Place the artichokes in the prepared basket. You may need to work in batches, depending on the size of your air fryer. 5. Air fry at 188ºC for 10 to 12 minutes, or until crispy and golden brown. 6. Sprinkle with the Parmesan cheese and season with salt and black pepper. Serve immediately.

Parmesan Cauliflower

Prep time: 15 minutes | Cook time: 15 minutes | Makes 5 cups

570 g small cauliflower florets
3 tablespoons olive oil
1 teaspoon garlic powder

½ teaspoon salt
½ teaspoon turmeric
30 g shredded Parmesan cheese

1. Preheat the air fryer to 200ºC. 2. In a bowl, combine the cauliflower florets, olive oil, garlic powder, salt, and turmeric and toss to coat. 3. Transfer to the air fryer basket and air fry for 15 minutes, or until the florets are crisp-tender. Shake the basket twice during cooking. 4. Remove from the basket to a plate. Sprinkle with the shredded Parmesan cheese and toss well. Serve warm.

Beef and Mango Skewers

Prep time: 10 minutes | Cook time: 4 to 7 minutes | Serves 4

340 g beef sirloin tip, cut into 1-inch cubes
2 tablespoons balsamic vinegar
1 tablespoon olive oil
1 tablespoon honey

½ teaspoon dried marjoram
Pinch of salt
Freshly ground black pepper, to taste
1 mango

1. Preheat the air fryer to 200ºC. 2. Put the beef cubes in a medium bowl and add the balsamic vinegar, olive oil, honey, marjoram, salt, and pepper. Mix well, then massage the marinade into the beef with your hands. Set aside. 3. To prepare the mango, stand it on end and cut the skin off, using a sharp knife. Then carefully cut around the oval pit to remove the flesh. Cut the mango into 1-inch cubes. 4. Thread metal skewers alternating with three beef cubes and two mango cubes. 5. Roast the skewers in the air fryer basket for 4 to 7 minutes, or until the beef is browned and at least 64ºC. 6. Serve hot.

Pickle Chips

Prep time: 30 minutes | Cook time: 12 minutes | Serves 4

Oil, for spraying
250 g sliced dill or sweet pickles, drained
250 ml buttermilk

250 g plain flour
2 large eggs, beaten
250 g panko bread crumbs
¼ teaspoon salt

1. Line the air fryer basket with baking paper and spray lightly with oil. 2. In a shallow bowl, combine the pickles and buttermilk and let soak for at least 1 hour, then drain. 3. Place the flour, beaten eggs, and bread crumbs in separate bowls. 4. Coat each pickle chip lightly in the flour, dip in the eggs, and dredge in the bread crumbs. Be sure each one is evenly coated. 5. Place the pickle chips in the prepared basket, sprinkle with the salt, and spray lightly with oil. You may need to work in batches, depending on the size of your air fryer. 6. Air fry at 200ºC for 5 minutes, flip, and cook for another 5 to 7 minutes, or until crispy. Serve hot.

Spinach and Crab Meat Cups

Prep time: 10 minutes | Cook time: 10 minutes | Makes 30 cups

1 (170 g) can crab meat, drained
5 g frozen spinach, thawed, drained, and chopped
1 clove garlic, minced
60 g grated Parmesan cheese
3 tablespoons plain yogurt

¼ teaspoon lemon juice
½ teaspoon Worcestershire sauce
30 mini frozen vol-au-vent cases, thawed
Cooking spray

1. Preheat the air fryer to 200ºC. 2. Remove any bits of shell that might remain in the crab meat. 3. Mix the crab meat, spinach, garlic, and cheese together. 4. Stir in the yogurt, lemon juice, and Worcestershire sauce and mix well. 5. Spoon a teaspoon of filling into each case. 6. Spray the air fryer basket with cooking spray and arrange half the cases in the basket. Air fry for 5 minutes. Repeat with the remaining cases. 7. Serve immediately.

Lemony Endive in Curried Yogurt

Prep time: 5 minutes | Cook time: 10 minutes | Serves 6

6 heads endive
125 ml plain and fat-free yogurt
3 tablespoons lemon juice
1 teaspoon garlic powder

½ teaspoon curry powder
Salt and ground black pepper, to taste

1. Wash the endives, and slice them in half lengthwise. 2. In a bowl, mix together the yogurt, lemon juice, garlic powder, curry powder, salt and pepper. 3. Brush the endive halves with the marinade, coating them completely. Allow to sit for at least 30 minutes or up to 24 hours. 4. Preheat the air fryer to 160ºC. 5. Put the endives in the air fryer basket and air fry for 10 minutes. 6. Serve hot.

Lemon-Pepper Chicken Drumsticks

Prep time: 30 minutes | Cook time: 30 minutes | Serves 2

2 teaspoons freshly ground coarse black pepper
1 teaspoon baking powder
½ teaspoon garlic powder
4 chicken drumsticks (115 g

each)
Kosher or coarse sea salt, to taste
1 lemon

1. In a small bowl, stir together the pepper, baking powder, and garlic powder. Place the drumsticks on a plate and sprinkle evenly with the baking powder mixture, turning the drumsticks so they're well coated. Let the drumsticks stand in the refrigerator for at least 1 hour or up to overnight. 2. Sprinkle the drumsticks with salt, then transfer them to the air fryer, standing them bone-end up and leaning against the wall of the air fryer basket. Air fry at 192ºC until cooked through and crisp on the outside, about 30 minutes. 3. Transfer the drumsticks to a serving platter and finely grate the zest of the lemon over them while they're hot. Cut the lemon into wedges and serve with the warm drumsticks.

Jalapeño Poppers

Prep time: 10 minutes | Cook time: 20 minutes | Serves 4

Oil, for spraying
230 g cream cheese
95 g gluten-free bread crumbs, divided
2 tablespoons chopped fresh

parsley
½ teaspoon granulated garlic
½ teaspoon salt
10 jalapeño peppers, halved and seeded

1. Line the air fryer basket with baking paper and spray lightly with oil. 2. In a medium bowl, mix together the cream cheese, half of the bread crumbs, the parsley, garlic, and salt. 3. Spoon the mixture into the jalapeño halves. Gently press the stuffed jalapeños in the remaining bread crumbs. 4. Place the stuffed jalapeños in the prepared basket. 5. Air fry at 188ºC for 20 minutes, or until the cheese is melted and the bread crumbs are crisp and golden brown.

Polenta Fries with Chilli-Lime Mayo

Prep time: 10 minutes | Cook time: 28 minutes | Serves 4

Polenta Fries:
2 teaspoons vegetable or olive oil
¼ teaspoon paprika
450 g prepared polenta, cut into 3-inch × ½-inch strips
Chilli-Lime Mayo:
125 g mayonnaise

1 teaspoon chilli powder
1 teaspoon chopped fresh coriander
¼ teaspoon ground cumin
Juice of ½ lime
Salt and freshly ground black pepper, to taste

1. Preheat the air fryer to 204°C. 2. Mix the oil and paprika in a bowl. Add the polenta strips and toss until evenly coated. 3. Transfer the polenta strips to the air fry basket and air fry for 28 minutes until the fries are golden brown, shaking the basket once during cooking. Season as desired with salt and pepper. 4. Meanwhile, whisk together all the ingredients for the chilli-lime mayo in a small bowl. 5. Remove the polenta fries from the air fryer to a plate and serve alongside the chilli-lime mayo as a dipping sauce.

Roasted Pearl Onion Dip

Prep time: 5 minutes | Cook time: 12 minutes | Serves 4

250 g peeled pearl onions
3 garlic cloves
3 tablespoons olive oil, divided
½ teaspoon salt
250 ml nonfat plain Greek yogurt

1 tablespoon lemon juice
¼ teaspoon black pepper
⅛ teaspoon red pepper flakes
Pita chips, vegetables, or toasted bread for serving (optional)

1. Preheat the air fryer to 180°C. 2. In a large bowl, combine the pearl onions and garlic with 2 tablespoons of the olive oil until the onions are well coated. 3. Pour the garlic-and-onion mixture into the air fryer basket and roast for 12 minutes. 4. Transfer the garlic and onions to a food processor. Pulse the vegetables several times, until the onions are minced but still have some chunks. 5. In a large bowl, combine the garlic and onions and the remaining 1 tablespoon of olive oil, along with the salt, yogurt, lemon juice, black pepper, and red pepper flakes. 6. Cover and chill for 1 hour before serving with pita chips, vegetables, or toasted bread.

Veggie Prawn Toast

Prep time: 15 minutes | Cook time: 3 to 6 minutes | Serves 4

8 large raw prawns, peeled and finely chopped
1 egg white
2 garlic cloves, minced
3 tablespoons minced red bell pepper

1 medium celery stalk, minced
2 tablespoons cornflour
¼ teaspoon Chinese five-spice powder
3 slices firm thin-sliced no-sodium whole-wheat bread

1. Preheat the air fryer to 176°C. 2. In a small bowl, stir together the prawns, egg white, garlic, red bell pepper, celery, cornflour, and

five-spice powder. Top each slice of bread with one-third of the prawn mixture, spreading it evenly to the edges. With a sharp knife, cut each slice of bread into 4 strips. 3. Place the prawn toasts in the air fryer basket in a single layer. You may need to cook them in batches. Air fry for 3 to 6 minutes, until crisp and golden brown. 4. Serve hot.

Authentic Scotch Eggs

Prep time: 15 minutes | Cook time: 11 to 13 minutes | Serves 6

680 g bulk lean chicken or turkey sausage
3 raw eggs, divided
185 g dried bread crumbs,

divided
60 g plain flour
6 hard boiled eggs, peeled
Cooking oil spray

1. In a large bowl, combine the chicken sausage, 1 raw egg, and 60 g bread crumbs and mix well. Divide the mixture into 6 pieces and flatten each into a long oval. 2. In a shallow bowl, beat the remaining 2 raw eggs. 3. Place the flour in a small bowl. 4. Place the remaining 125 g bread crumbs in a second small bowl. 5. Roll each hardboiled egg in the flour and wrap one of the chicken sausage pieces around each egg to encircle it completely. 6. One at a time, roll the encased eggs in the flour, dip in the beaten eggs, and finally dip in the bread crumbs to coat. 7. Insert the crisper plate into the basket and the basket into the unit. Preheat the unit by selecting AIR FRY, setting the temperature to 192°C, and setting the time to 3 minutes. Select START/STOP to begin. 8. Once the unit is preheated, spray the crisper plate with cooking oil. Place the eggs in a single layer into the basket and spray them with oil. 9. Select AIR FRY, set the temperature to 192°C, and set the time to 13 minutes. Select START/STOP to begin. 10. After about 6 minutes, use tongs to turn the eggs and spray them with more oil. Resume cooking for 5 to 7 minutes more, or until the chicken is thoroughly cooked and the Scotch eggs are browned. 11. When the cooking is complete, serve warm.

Greek Street Tacos

Prep time: 10 minutes | Cook time: 3 minutes | Makes 8 small tacos

8 small flour tortillas (4-inch diameter)
8 tablespoons hummus
4 tablespoons crumbled feta cheese

4 tablespoons chopped Kalamata or other olives (optional)
Olive oil for misting

1. Place 1 tablespoon of hummus or tapenade in the center of each tortilla. Top with 1 teaspoon of feta crumbles and 1 teaspoon of chopped olives, if using. 2. Using your finger or a small spoon, moisten the edges of the tortilla all around with water. 3. Fold tortilla over to make a half-moon shape. Press center gently. Then press the edges firmly to seal in the filling. 4. Mist both sides with olive oil. 5. Place in air fryer basket very close but try not to overlap. 6. Air fry at 200°C for 3 minutes, just until lightly browned and crispy.

Cream Cheese Wontons

Prep time: 15 minutes | Cook time: 6 minutes | Makes 20 wontons

Oil, for spraying
20 wonton wrappers
115 g cream cheese

1. Line the air fryer basket with baking paper and spray lightly with oil. 2. Pour some water in a small bowl. 3. Lay out a wonton wrapper and place 1 teaspoon of cream cheese in the center. 4. Dip your finger in the water and moisten the edge of the wonton wrapper. Fold over the opposite corners to make a triangle and press the edges together. 5. Pinch the corners of the triangle together to form a classic wonton shape. Place the wonton in the prepared basket. Repeat with the remaining wrappers and cream cheese. You may need to work in batches, depending on the size of your air fryer. 6. Air fry at 204°C for 6 minutes, or until golden brown around the edges.

Buffalo Bites

Prep time: 15 minutes | Cook time: 11 to 12 minutes per batch | Makes 16 meatballs

185 g cooked jasmine or sushi rice
¼ teaspoon salt
450 g minced chicken
8 tablespoons buffalo wing sauce
60 g Gruyère cheese, cut into 16 cubes
1 tablespoon maple syrup

1. Mix 4 tablespoons buffalo wing sauce into all the minced chicken. 2. Shape chicken into a log and divide into 16 equal portions. 3. With slightly damp hands, mold each chicken portion around a cube of cheese and shape into a firm ball. When you have shaped 8 meatballs, place them in air fryer basket. 4. Air fry at 200°C for approximately 5 minutes. Shake basket, reduce temperature to 180°C, and cook for 5 to 6 minutes longer. 5. While the first batch is cooking, shape remaining chicken and cheese into 8 more meatballs. 6. Repeat step 4 to cook second batch of meatballs. 7. In a medium bowl, mix the remaining 4 tablespoons of buffalo wing sauce with the maple syrup. Add all the cooked meatballs and toss to coat. 8. Place meatballs back into air fryer basket and air fry at 200°C for 2 to 3 minutes to set the glaze. Skewer each with a toothpick and serve.

Aubergine Fries

Prep time: 10 minutes | Cook time: 7 to 8 minutes per batch | Serves 4

1 medium aubergine
1 teaspoon ground coriander
1 teaspoon cumin
1 teaspoon garlic powder
½ teaspoon salt
125 g crushed panko bread crumbs
1 large egg
2 tablespoons water
Oil for misting or cooking spray

1. Peel and cut the aubergine into fat fries, ⅜- to ½-inch thick. 2. Preheat the air fryer to 200°C. 3. In a small cup, mix together the coriander, cumin, garlic, and salt. 4. Combine 1 teaspoon of the seasoning mix and panko crumbs in a shallow dish. 5. Place aubergine fries in a large bowl, sprinkle with remaining seasoning, and stir well to combine. 6. Beat eggs and water together and pour over aubergine fries. Stir to coat. 7. Remove aubergine from egg wash, shaking off excess, and roll in panko crumbs. 8. Spray with oil. 9. Place half of the fries in air fryer basket. You should have only a single layer, but it's fine if they overlap a little. 10. Cook for 5 minutes. Shake basket, mist lightly with oil, and cook 2 to 3 minutes longer, until browned and crispy. 11. Repeat step 10 to cook remaining eggplant.

Shishito Peppers with Herb Dressing

Prep time: 10 minutes | Cook time: 6 minutes | Serves 2 to 4

170 g Shishito peppers
1 tablespoon vegetable oil
Kosher or coarse sea salt and freshly ground black pepper, to taste
125 g mayonnaise
2 tablespoons finely chopped fresh basil leaves
2 tablespoons finely chopped
fresh flat-leaf parsley
1 tablespoon finely chopped fresh tarragon
1 tablespoon finely chopped fresh chives
Finely grated zest of ½ lemon
1 tablespoon fresh lemon juice
Flaky sea salt, for serving

1. Preheat the air fryer to 204°C. 2. In a bowl, toss together the Shishitos and oil to evenly coat and season with kosher salt and black pepper. Transfer to the air fryer and air fry for 6 minutes, shaking the basket halfway through, or until the Shishitos are blistered and lightly charred. 3. Meanwhile, in a small bowl, whisk together the mayonnaise, basil, parsley, tarragon, chives, lemon zest, and lemon juice. 4. Pile the peppers on a plate, sprinkle with flaky sea salt, and serve hot with the dressing.

Courgette Feta Roulades

Prep time: 10 minutes | Cook time: 10 minutes | Serves 6

60 g feta
1 garlic clove, minced
2 tablespoons fresh basil, minced
1 tablespoon capers, minced
⅛ teaspoon salt
⅛ teaspoon red pepper flakes
1 tablespoon lemon juice
2 medium courgette
12 toothpicks

1. Preheat the air fryer to 180°C (If using a grill attachment, make sure it is inside the air fryer during preheating). 2. In a small bowl, combine the feta, garlic, basil, capers, salt, red pepper flakes, and lemon juice. 3. Slice the courgette into ⅛-inch strips lengthwise. (Each courgette should yield around 6 strips.) 4. Spread 1 tablespoon of the cheese filling onto each slice of courgette, then roll it up and secure it with a toothpick through the middle. 5. Place the courgette roulades into the air fryer basket in a single layer, making sure that they don't touch each other. 6. Bake or grill in the air fryer for 10 minutes. 7. Remove the courgette roulades from the air fryer and gently remove the toothpicks before serving.

Crispy Breaded Beef Cubes

Prep time: 10 minutes | Cook time: 12 to 16 minutes | Serves 4

450 g sirloin tip, cut into 1-inch cubes
250 g cheese pasta sauce
185 g soft bread crumbs

2 tablespoons olive oil
½ teaspoon dried marjoram

1. Preheat the air fryer to 180ºC. 2. In a medium bowl, toss the beef with the pasta sauce to coat. 3. In a shallow bowl, combine the bread crumbs, oil, and marjoram, and mix well. Drop the beef cubes, one at a time, into the bread crumb mixture to coat thoroughly. 4. Air fry the beef in two batches for 6 to 8 minutes, shaking the basket once during cooking time, until the beef is at least 64ºC and the outside is crisp and brown. 5. Serve hot.

Carrot Chips

Prep time: 15 minutes | Cook time: 8 to 10 minutes | Serves 4

1 tablespoon olive oil, plus more for greasing the basket
4 to 5 medium carrots, trimmed and thinly sliced

1 teaspoon seasoned salt

1. Preheat the air fryer to 200ºC. Grease the air fryer basket with the olive oil. 2. Toss the carrot slices with 1 tablespoon of olive oil and salt in a medium bowl until thoroughly coated. 3. Arrange the carrot slices in the greased basket. You may need to work in batches to avoid overcrowding. 4. Air fry for 8 to 10 minutes until the carrot slices are crisp-tender. Shake the basket once during cooking. 5. Transfer the carrot slices to a bowl and repeat with the remaining carrots. 6. Allow to cool for 5 minutes and serve.

Crunchy Tex-Mex Tortilla Chips

Prep time: 5 minutes | Cook time: 5 minutes | Serves 4

Olive oil
½ teaspoon salt
½ teaspoon ground cumin
½ teaspoon chilli powder

½ teaspoon paprika
Pinch cayenne pepper
8 (6-inch) corn tortillas, each cut into 6 wedges

1. Spray fryer basket lightly with olive oil. 2. In a small bowl, combine the salt, cumin, chilli powder, paprika, and cayenne pepper. 3. Place the tortilla wedges in the air fryer basket in a single layer. Spray the tortillas lightly with oil and sprinkle with some of the seasoning mixture. You will need to cook the tortillas in batches. 4. Air fry at 192ºC for 2 to 3 minutes. Shake the basket and cook until the chips are light brown and crispy, an additional 2 to 3 minutes. Watch the chips closely so they do not burn.

Chapter 8 Desserts

Chapter 8 Desserts

Chocolate and Rum Cupcakes

Prep time: 5 minutes | Cook time: 15 minutes | Serves 6

95 g granulated sweetener
155 g almond flour
1 teaspoon unsweetened baking powder
3 teaspoons cocoa powder
½ teaspoon baking soda
½ teaspoon ground cinnamon
¼ teaspoon grated nutmeg
⅛ teaspoon salt

125 ml milk
1 stick butter, at room temperature
3 eggs, whisked
1 teaspoon pure rum extract or apple juice
60 g blueberries
Cooking spray

1. Preheat the air fryer to 172ºC. Spray a 6-cup muffin tin with cooking spray. 2. In a mixing bowl, combine the sweetener, almond flour, baking powder, cocoa powder, baking soda, cinnamon, nutmeg, and salt and stir until well blended. 3. In another mixing bowl, mix together the milk, butter, egg, and rum extract until thoroughly combined. Slowly and carefully pour this mixture into the bowl of dry mixture. Stir in the blueberries. 4. Spoon the batter into the greased muffin cups, filling each about three-quarters full. 5. Bake for 15 minutes, or until the center is springy and a toothpick inserted in the middle comes out clean. 6. Remove from the basket and place on a wire rack to cool. Serve immediately.

Molten Chocolate Almond Cakes

Prep time: 5 minutes | Cook time: 13 minutes | Serves 3

Butter and flour for the ramekins
115 g bittersweet chocolate, chopped
125 g unsalted butter
2 eggs
2 egg yolks
30 g sugar
½ teaspoon pure vanilla extract, or almond extract

1 tablespoon plain flour
3 tablespoons ground almonds
8 to 12 semisweet chocolate discs (or 4 chunks of chocolate)
Cocoa powder or icing sugar, for dusting
Toasted almonds, coarsely chopped

1. Butter and flour three (170 g) ramekins. (Butter the ramekins and then coat the butter with flour by shaking it around in the ramekin and dumping out any excess.) 2. Melt the chocolate and butter together, either in the microwave or in a double boiler. In a separate bowl, beat the eggs, egg yolks and sugar together until light and smooth. Add the vanilla extract. Whisk the chocolate mixture into the egg mixture. Stir in the flour and ground almonds. 3. Preheat the air fryer to 164ºC. 4. Transfer the batter carefully to the buttered ramekins, filling halfway. Place two or three chocolate discs in the center of the batter and then fill the ramekins to ½-inch below the top with the remaining batter. Place the ramekins into the air fryer basket and air fry at 164ºC for 13 minutes. The sides of the cake should be set, but the centers should be slightly soft. Remove the ramekins from the air fryer and let the cakes sit for 5 minutes. (If you'd like the cake a little less molten, air fry for 14 minutes and let the cakes sit for 4 minutes.) 5. Run a butter knife around the edge of the ramekins and invert the cakes onto a plate. Lift the ramekin off the plate slowly and carefully so that the cake doesn't break. Dust with cocoa powder or icing sugar and serve with a scoop of ice cream and some coarsely chopped toasted almonds.

Pumpkin Pudding with Vanilla Wafers

Prep time: 10 minutes | Cook time: 12 to 17 minutes | Serves 4

250 g canned no-salt-added pumpkin purée (not pumpkin pie filling)
30 g packed brown sugar
3 tablespoons plain flour
1 egg, whisked
2 tablespoons milk

1 tablespoon unsalted butter, melted
1 teaspoon pure vanilla extract
4 low-fat vanilla wafers, crumbled
Nonstick cooking spray

1. Preheat the air fryer to 176ºC. Coat a baking pan with nonstick cooking spray. Set aside. 2. Mix the pumpkin purée, brown sugar, flour, whisked egg, milk, melted butter, and vanilla in a medium bowl and whisk to combine. Transfer the mixture to the baking pan. 3. Place the baking pan in the air fryer basket and bake for 12 to 17 minutes until set. 4. Remove the pudding from the basket to a wire rack to cool. 5. Divide the pudding into four bowls and serve with the vanilla wafers sprinkled on top.

Fried Cheesecake Bites

Prep time: 30 minutes | Cook time: 2 minutes | Makes 16 bites

230 g cream cheese, softened
90 g powdered sweetener, divided
4 tablespoons heavy cream,

divided
½ teaspoon vanilla extract
60 g almond flour

1. In a stand mixer fitted with a paddle attachment, beat the cream cheese, 60 g sweetener, 2 tablespoons of the heavy cream, and the vanilla until smooth. Using a small ice-cream scoop, divide the mixture into 16 balls and arrange them on a rimmed baking sheet lined with baking paper. Freeze for 45 minutes until firm. 2. Line the air fryer basket with baking paper and preheat the air fryer to 176ºC. 3. In a small shallow bowl, combine the almond flour with the remaining 2 tablespoons sweetener. 4. In another small shallow bowl, place the remaining 2 tablespoons cream. 5. One at a time, dip the frozen cheesecake balls into the cream and then roll in the almond flour mixture, pressing lightly to form an even coating. Arrange the balls in a single layer in the air fryer basket, leaving room between them. Air fry for 2 minutes until the coating is lightly browned.

Pumpkin-Spice Bread Pudding

Prep time: 15 minutes | Cook time: 35 minutes | Serves 6

Bread Pudding:
190 g heavy whipping cream
60 g canned pumpkin
85 ml whole milk
40 g sugar
1 large egg plus 1 yolk
½ teaspoon pumpkin pie spice
⅛ teaspoon kosher or coarse sea salt

500 g 1-inch cubed day-old baguette or crusty country bread
4 tablespoons unsalted butter, melted
Sauce:
80 g pure maple syrup
1 tablespoon unsalted butter
125 g heavy whipping cream
½ teaspoon pure vanilla extract

1. For the bread pudding: In a medium bowl, combine the cream, pumpkin, milk, sugar, egg and yolk, pumpkin pie spice, and salt. Whisk until well combined. 2. In a large bowl, toss the bread cubes with the melted butter. Add the pumpkin mixture and gently toss until the ingredients are well combined. 3. Transfer the mixture to a baking pan. Place the pan in the air fryer basket. Set the fryer to 176ºC for 35 minutes, or until custard is set in the middle. 4. Meanwhile, for the sauce: In a small saucepan, combine the syrup and butter. Heat over medium heat, stirring, until the butter melts. Stir in the cream and simmer, stirring often, until the sauce has thickened, about 15 minutes. Stir in the vanilla. Remove the pudding from the air fryer. 5. Let the pudding stand for 10 minutes before serving with the warm sauce.

Halle Berries-and-Cream Cobbler

Prep time: 10 minutes | Cook time: 25 minutes | Serves 4

340 g cream cheese, softened
1 large egg
95 g Powdered sweetener
½ teaspoon vanilla extract
¼ teaspoon fine sea salt
125 g sliced fresh raspberries or strawberries
Biscuits:
3 large egg whites
95 g blanched almond flour
1 teaspoon baking powder
2½ tablespoons very cold

unsalted butter, cut into pieces
¼ teaspoon fine sea salt
Frosting:
60 g cream cheese, softened
1 tablespoon of powdered or liquid sweetener
1 tablespoon unsweetened, unflavored almond milk or heavy cream
Fresh raspberries or strawberries, for garnish

1. Preheat the air fryer to 204ºC. Grease a pie pan. 2. In a large mixing bowl, use a hand mixer to combine the cream cheese, egg, and sweetener until smooth. Stir in the vanilla and salt. Gently fold in the raspberries with a rubber spatula. Pour the mixture into the prepared pan and set aside. 3. Make the biscuits: Place the egg whites in a medium-sized mixing bowl or the bowl of a stand mixer. Using a hand mixer or stand mixer, whip the egg whites until very fluffy and stiff. 4. In a separate medium-sized bowl, combine the almond flour and baking powder. Cut in the butter and add the salt, stirring gently to keep the butter pieces intact. 5. Gently fold the almond flour mixture into the egg whites. Use a large spoon or ice cream scooper to scoop out the dough and form it into a 2-inch-wide biscuit, making sure the butter stays in separate clumps. Place the biscuit on top of the raspberry mixture in the pan. Repeat with remaining dough to make 4 biscuits. 6. Place the pan

in the air fryer and bake for 5 minutes, then lower the temperature to 164ºC and bake for another 17 to 20 minutes, until the biscuits are golden brown. 7. While the cobbler cooks, make the frosting: Place the cream cheese in a small bowl and stir to break it up. Add the sweetener and stir. Add the almond milk and stir until well combined. If you prefer a thinner frosting, add more almond milk. 8. Remove the cobbler from the air fryer and allow to cool slightly, then drizzle with the frosting. Garnish with fresh raspberries. 9. Store leftovers in an airtight container in the refrigerator for up to 3 days. Reheat the cobbler in a preheated 176ºC air fryer for 3 minutes, or until warmed through.

5-Ingredient Brownies

Prep time: 10 minutes | Cook time: 25 minutes | Serves 6

Vegetable oil
125 g unsalted butter
60 g chocolate chips

3 large eggs
60 g sugar
1 teaspoon pure vanilla extract

1. Generously grease a baking pan with vegetable oil. 2. In a microwave-safe bowl, combine the butter and chocolate chips. Microwave on high for 1 minute. Stir very well. (You want the heat from the butter and chocolate to melt the remaining clumps. If you microwave until everything melts, the chocolate will be overcooked. If necessary, microwave for an additional 10 seconds, but stir well before you try that.) 3. In a medium bowl, combine the eggs, sugar, and vanilla. Whisk until light and frothy. While whisking continuously, slowly pour in the melted chocolate in a thin stream and whisk until everything is incorporated. 4. Pour the batter into the prepared pan. Set the pan in the air fryer basket. Set the air fryer to 176ºC for 25 minutes, or until a toothpick inserted into the center comes out clean. 5. Let cool in the pan on a wire rack for 30 minutes before cutting into squares.

Indian Toast and Milk

Prep time: 10 minutes | Cook time: 20 minutes | Serves 4

250 ml sweetened condensed milk
250 ml evaporated milk
250 ml single cream
1 teaspoon ground cardamom, plus additional for garnish

1 pinch saffron threads
4 slices white bread
2 to 3 tablespoons ghee or butter, softened
2 tablespoons crushed pistachios, for garnish (optional)

1. In a baking pan, combine the condensed milk, evaporated milk, single cream, cardamom, and saffron. Stir until well combined. 2. Place the pan in the air fryer basket. Set the air fryer to 176ºC for 15 minutes, stirring halfway through the cooking time. Remove the sweetened milk from the air fryer and set aside. 3. Cut each slice of bread into two triangles. Brush each side with ghee. Place the bread in the air fryer basket. Set the air fryer to 176ºC for 5 minutes or until golden brown and toasty. 4. Remove the bread from the air fryer. Arrange two triangles in each of four wide, shallow bowls. Pour the hot milk mixture on top of the bread and let soak for 30 minutes. 5. Garnish with pistachios if using, and sprinkle with additional cardamom.

Pecan Bars

Prep time: 5 minutes | Cook time: 40 minutes | Serves 12

250 g coconut flour	softened
5 tablespoons granulated sweetener	125 g heavy cream
	1 egg, beaten
4 tablespoons coconut oil,	4 pecans, chopped

1. Mix coconut flour, sweetener, coconut oil, heavy cream, and egg. 2. Pour the batter in the air fryer basket and flatten well. 3. Top the mixture with pecans and cook the meal at 176°C for 40 minutes. 4. Cut the cooked meal into the bars.

Lemon Poppy Seed Macaroons

Prep time: 10 minutes | Cook time: 14 minutes | Makes 1 dozen cookies

2 large egg whites, room temperature	¼ teaspoon fine sea salt
40 g powdered sweetener	250 g unsweetened desiccated coconut
2 tablespoons grated lemon zest, plus more for garnish if desired	Lemon Icing:
2 teaspoons poppy seeds	30 g powdered sweetener
1 teaspoon lemon extract	1 tablespoon lemon juice

1. Preheat the air fryer to 164°C. Line a pie pan or a casserole dish that will fit inside your air fryer with baking paper. 2. Place the egg whites in a medium-sized bowl and use a hand mixer on high to beat the whites until stiff peaks form. Add the sweetener, lemon zest, poppy seeds, lemon extract, and salt. Mix on low until combined. Gently fold in the coconut with a rubber spatula. 3. Use a 1-inch cookie scoop to place the cookies on the baking paper, spacing them about ¼ inch apart. Place the pan in the air fryer and bake for 12 to 14 minutes, until the cookies are golden and a toothpick inserted into the center comes out clean. 4. While the cookies bake, make the lemon icing: Place the sweetener in a small bowl. Add the lemon juice and stir well. If the icing is too thin, add a little more sweetener. If the icing is too thick, add a little more lemon juice. 5. Remove the cookies from the air fryer and allow to cool for about 10 minutes, then drizzle with the icing. Garnish with lemon zest, if desired. Store leftovers in an airtight container in the fridge for up to 5 days or in the freezer for up to a month.

S'mores

Prep time: 5 minutes | Cook time: 30 seconds | Makes 8 s'mores

Oil, for spraying	2 (40 g) chocolate bars
8 digestive biscuits	4 large marshmallows

1. Line the air fryer basket with baking paper and spray lightly with oil. 2. Place 4 digestive biscuits in the prepared basket. 3. Break the chocolate bars in half and place 1 piece on top of each biscuit. Top with 1 marshmallow. 4. Air fry at 188°C for 30 seconds, or until the marshmallows are puffed and golden brown and slightly melted. 5. Top with the remaining biscuits and serve.

Cream-Filled Sandwich Cookies

Prep time: 8 minutes | Cook time: 8 minutes | Makes 8 cookies

Oil, for spraying	60 ml milk
230 g ready-made croissant dough	8 cream-filled sandwich cookies
	1 tablespoon icing sugar

1. Line the air fryer basket with baking paper and spray lightly with oil. 2. Unroll the croissant dough and separate it into 8 triangles. Lay out the triangles on a work surface. 3. Pour the milk into a shallow bowl. Quickly dip each cookie in the milk, then place in the center of a dough triangle. 4. Wrap the dough around the cookie, cutting off any excess and pinching the ends to seal. You may be able to combine the excess into enough dough to cover additional cookies, if desired. 5. Place the wrapped cookies in the prepared basket, seam-side down, and spray lightly with oil. 6. Bake at 176°C for 4 minutes, flip, spray with oil, and cook for another 3 to 4 minutes, or until puffed and golden brown. 7. Dust with the icing sugar and serve.

Peanut Butter-Honey-Banana Toast

Prep time: 10 minutes | Cook time: 9 minutes | Serves 4

2 tablespoons butter, softened	sliced
4 slices white bread	4 tablespoons honey
4 tablespoons peanut butter	1 teaspoon ground cinnamon
2 bananas, peeled and thinly	

1. Spread butter on one side of each slice of bread, then peanut butter on the other side. Arrange the banana slices on top of the peanut butter sides of each slice (about 9 slices per toast). Drizzle honey on top of the banana and sprinkle with cinnamon. 2. Cut each slice in half lengthwise so that it will better fit into the air fryer basket. Arrange two pieces of bread, butter sides down, in the air fryer basket. Set the air fryer to 192°C for 5 minutes. Then set the air fryer to 204°C for an additional 4 minutes, or until the bananas have started to brown. Repeat with remaining slices. Serve hot.

Protein Powder Doughnut Holes

Prep time: 25 minutes | Cook time: 6 minutes | Makes 12 holes

60 g blanched finely ground almond flour	½ teaspoon baking powder
	1 large egg
60 g low-carb vanilla protein powder	5 tablespoons unsalted butter, melted
60 g granulated sweetener	½ teaspoon vanilla extract

1. Mix all ingredients in a large bowl. Place into the freezer for 20 minutes. 2. Wet your hands with water and roll the dough into twelve balls. 3. Cut a piece of baking paper to fit your air fryer basket. Working in batches as necessary, place doughnut holes into the air fryer basket on top of baking paper. 4. Adjust the temperature to 192°C and air fry for 6 minutes. 5. Flip doughnut holes halfway through the cooking time. 6. Let cool completely before serving.

Double Chocolate Brownies

Prep time: 5 minutes | Cook time: 15 to 20 minutes | Serves 8

125 g almond flour
60 g unsweetened cocoa powder
½ teaspoon baking powder
40 g powdered sweetener
¼ teaspoon salt
125 g unsalted butter, melted
and cooled
3 eggs
1 teaspoon vanilla extract
2 tablespoons mini semisweet chocolate chips

1. Preheat the air fryer to 176ºC. Line a cake pan with baking paper and brush with oil. 2. In a large bowl, combine the almond flour, cocoa powder, baking powder, sweetener, and salt. Add the butter, eggs, and vanilla. Stir until thoroughly combined. (The batter will be thick.) Spread the batter into the prepared pan and scatter the chocolate chips on top. 3. Air fry for 15 to 20 minutes until the edges are set. (The center should still appear slightly undercooked.) Let cool completely before slicing. To store, cover and refrigerate the brownies for up to 3 days.

Pecan Butter Cookies

Prep time: 5 minutes | Cook time: 24 minutes | Makes 12 cookies

125 g chopped pecans
125 g salted butter, melted
60 g coconut flour
95 g granulated sweetener, divided
1 teaspoon vanilla extract

1. In a food processor, blend together pecans, butter, flour, 60 g sweetener, and vanilla 1 minute until a dough forms. 2. Form dough into twelve individual cookie balls, about 1 tablespoon each. 3. Cut three pieces of baking paper to fit air fryer basket. Place four cookies on each ungreased baking paper and place one piece baking paper with cookies into air fryer basket. Adjust air fryer temperature to 164ºC and set the timer for 8 minutes. Repeat cooking with remaining batches. 4. When the timer goes off, allow cookies to cool 5 minutes on a large serving plate until cool enough to handle. While still warm, dust cookies with remaining sweetener. Allow to cool completely, about 15 minutes, before serving.

Cardamom Custard

Prep time: 10 minutes | Cook time: 25 minutes | Serves 2

250 ml whole milk
1 large egg
2 tablespoons plus 1 teaspoon sugar
¼ teaspoon vanilla bean paste or pure vanilla extract
¼ teaspoon ground cardamom, plus more for sprinkling

1. In a medium bowl, beat together the milk, egg, sugar, vanilla, and cardamom. 2. Place two 230 g ramekins in the air fryer basket. Divide the mixture between the ramekins. Sprinkle lightly with cardamom. Cover each ramekin tightly with aluminum foil. Set the air fryer to 176ºC for 25 minutes, or until a toothpick inserted in the center comes out clean. 3. Let the custards cool on a wire rack for 5 to 10 minutes. 4. Serve warm, or refrigerate until cold and serve chilled.

Butter Flax Cookies

Prep time: 25 minutes | Cook time: 20 minutes | Serves 4

230 g almond meal
2 tablespoons flaxseed meal
30 g monk fruit
1 teaspoon baking powder
A pinch of grated nutmeg
A pinch of coarse salt
1 large egg, room temperature.
115 g butter, room temperature
1 teaspoon vanilla extract

1. Mix the almond meal, flaxseed meal, monk fruit, baking powder, grated nutmeg, and salt in a bowl. 2. In a separate bowl, whisk the egg, butter, and vanilla extract. 3. Stir the egg mixture into dry mixture; mix to combine well or until it forms a nice, soft dough. 4. Roll your dough out and cut out with a cookie cutter of your choice. Bake in the preheated air fryer at 176ºC for 10 minutes. Decrease the temperature to 164ºC and cook for 10 minutes longer. Bon appétit!

Coconut Macaroons

Prep time: 5 minutes | Cook time: 8 to 10 minutes | Makes 12 macaroons

165 g sweetened, desiccated coconut
4½ teaspoons almond flour
2 tablespoons sugar
1 egg white
½ teaspoon almond extract

1. Preheat the air fryer to 164ºC. 2. Mix all ingredients together. 3. Shape coconut mixture into 12 balls. 4. Place all 12 macaroons in air fryer basket. They won't expand, so you can place them close together, but they shouldn't touch. 5. Air fry at 164ºC for 8 to 10 minutes, until golden.

Roasted Honey Pears

Prep time: 7 minutes | Cook time: 18 to 23 minutes | Serves 4

2 large Bosc pears, halved lengthwise and seeded
3 tablespoons honey
1 tablespoon unsalted butter
½ teaspoon ground cinnamon
30 g walnuts, chopped
30 g part-skim ricotta cheese, divided

1. Insert the crisper plate into the basket and the basket into the unit. Preheat the unit by selecting AIR ROAST, setting the temperature to 176ºC, and setting the time to 3 minutes. Select START/STOP to begin. 2. In a 6-by-2-inch round pan, place the pears cut-side up. 3. In a small microwave-safe bowl, melt the honey, butter, and cinnamon. Brush this mixture over the cut sides of the pears. Pour 3 tablespoons of water around the pears in the pan. 4. Once the unit is preheated, place the pan into the basket. 5. Select AIR ROAST, set the temperature to 176ºC, and set the time to 23 minutes. Select START/STOP to begin. 6. After about 18 minutes, check the pears. They should be tender when pierced with a fork and slightly crisp on the edges. If not, resume cooking. 7. When the cooking is complete, baste the pears once with the liquid in the pan. Carefully remove the pears from the pan and place on a serving plate. Drizzle each with some liquid from the pan, sprinkle the walnuts on top, and serve with a spoonful of ricotta cheese.

Chickpea Brownies

Prep time: 10 minutes | Cook time: 20 minutes | Serves 6

Vegetable oil
1 (425 g) can chickpeas, drained and rinsed
4 large eggs
85 ml coconut oil, melted
80 g honey
3 tablespoons unsweetened

cocoa powder
1 tablespoon espresso powder (optional)
1 teaspoon baking powder
1 teaspoon baking soda
60 g chocolate chips

1. Preheat the air fryer to 164°C. 2. Generously grease a baking pan with vegetable oil. 3. In a blender or food processor, combine the chickpeas, eggs, coconut oil, honey, cocoa powder, espresso powder (if using), baking powder, and baking soda. Blend or process until smooth. Transfer to the prepared pan and stir in the chocolate chips by hand. 4. Set the pan in the air fryer basket and bake for 20 minutes, or until a toothpick inserted into the center comes out clean. 5. Let cool in the pan on a wire rack for 30 minutes before cutting into squares. 6. Serve immediately.

Nutty Pear Crumble

Prep time: 10 minutes | Cook time: 30 minutes | Serves 2 to 4

2 ripe d'Anjou pears (450 g), peeled, cored, and roughly chopped
30 g packed light brown sugar
2 tablespoons cornflour
1 teaspoon kosher or coarse sea salt
30 g granulated sugar
3 tablespoons unsalted butter, at

room temperature
40 g plain flour
2½ tablespoons Dutch-process cocoa powder
30 g chopped blanched hazelnuts
Vanilla ice cream or whipped cream, for serving (optional)

1. In a cake pan, combine the pears, brown sugar, cornflour, and ½ teaspoon salt and toss until the pears are evenly coated in the sugar. 2. In a bowl, combine the remaining ½ teaspoon salt with the granulated sugar, butter, flour, and cocoa powder and pinch and press the butter into the other ingredients with your fingers until a sandy, shaggy crumble dough forms. Stir in the hazelnuts. Sprinkle the crumble topping evenly over the pears. 3. Place the pan in the air fryer and bake at 160°C until the crumble is crisp and the pears are bubbling in the center, about 30 minutes. 4. Carefully remove the pan from the air fryer and serve the hot crumble in bowls, topped with ice cream or whipped cream, if you like.

Simple Pineapple Sticks

Prep time: 5 minutes | Cook time: 10 minutes | Serves 4

½ fresh pineapple, cut into sticks
30 g desiccated coconut

1. Preheat the air fryer to 204°C. 2. Coat the pineapple sticks in the desiccated coconut and put each one in the air fryer basket. 3. Air fry for 10 minutes. 4. Serve immediately

Cream Cheese Danish

Prep time: 20 minutes | Cook time: 15 minutes | Serves 6

95 g blanched finely ground almond flour
125 g shredded Mozzarella cheese
140 g full-fat cream cheese, divided

2 large egg yolks
95 g Powdered sweetener, divided
2 teaspoons vanilla extract, divided

1. In a large microwave-safe bowl, add almond flour, Mozzarella, and 30 g cream cheese. Mix and then microwave for 1 minute. 2. Stir and add egg yolks to the bowl. Continue stirring until soft dough forms. Add 60 g sweetener to dough and 1 teaspoon vanilla. 3. Cut a piece of baking paper to fit your air fryer basket. Wet your hands with warm water and press out the dough into a ¼-inch-thick rectangle. 4. In a medium bowl, mix remaining cream cheese, sweetener, and vanilla. Place this cream cheese mixture on the right half of the dough rectangle. Fold over the left side of the dough and press to seal. Place into the air fryer basket. 5. Adjust the temperature to 164°C and bake for 15 minutes. 6. After 7 minutes, flip over the Danish. 7. When done, remove the Danish from baking paper and allow to completely cool before cutting.

Strawberry Pastry Rolls

Prep time: 20 minutes | Cook time: 5 to 6 minutes per batch | Serves 4

85 g low-fat cream cheese
2 tablespoons plain yogurt
2 teaspoons sugar
¼ teaspoon pure vanilla extract
230 g fresh strawberries

8 sheets filo pastry
Butter-flavored cooking spray
50 g dark chocolate chips (optional)

1. In a medium bowl, combine the cream cheese, yogurt, sugar, and vanilla. Beat with hand mixer at high speed until smooth, about 1 minute. 2. Wash strawberries and destem. Chop enough of them to measure 60 g. Stir into cheese mixture. 3. Preheat the air fryer to 164°C. 4. Filo pastry dries out quickly, so cover your stack of filo sheets with waxed paper and then place a damp dish towel on top of that. Remove only one sheet at a time as you work. 5. To create one pastry roll, lay out a single sheet of filo. Spray lightly with butter-flavored spray, top with a second sheet of filo, and spray the second sheet lightly. 6. Place a quarter of the filling (about 3 tablespoons) about ½ inch from the edge of one short side. Fold the end of the filo over the filling and keep rolling a turn or two. Fold in both the left and right sides so that the edges meet in the middle of your roll. Then roll up completely. Spray outside of pastry roll with butter spray. 7. When you have 4 rolls, place them in the air fryer basket, seam side down, leaving some space in between each. Air fry at 164°C for 5 to 6 minutes, until they turn a delicate golden brown. 8. Repeat step 7 for remaining rolls. 9. Allow pastries to cool to room temperature. 10. When ready to serve, slice the remaining strawberries. If desired, melt the chocolate chips in microwave or double boiler. Place 1 pastry on each dessert plate, and top with sliced strawberries. Drizzle melted chocolate over strawberries and onto plate.

Fried Oreos

Prep time: 7 minutes | Cook time: 6 minutes per batch | Makes 12 cookies

Oil for misting or nonstick spray	12 Oreos or other chocolate
125 g complete pancake mix	sandwich cookies
1 teaspoon vanilla extract	1 tablespoon confectioners'
150 ml water	sugar

1. Spray baking pan with oil or nonstick spray and place in basket. 2. Preheat the air fryer to 200°C. 3. In a medium bowl, mix together the pancake mix, vanilla, and water. 4. Dip 4 cookies in batter and place in baking pan. 5. Cook for 6 minutes, until browned. 6. Repeat steps 4 and 5 for the remaining cookies. 7. Sift sugar over warm cookies.

Pretzels

Prep time: 10 minutes | Cook time: 10 minutes | Serves 6

185 g shredded Mozzarella cheese	melted, divided
125 g blanched finely ground almond flour	30 g granulated sweetener, divided
2 tablespoons salted butter,	1 teaspoon ground cinnamon

1. Place Mozzarella, flour, 1 tablespoon butter, and 2 tablespoons sweetener in a large microwave-safe bowl. Microwave on high 45 seconds, then stir with a fork until a smooth dough ball forms. 2. Separate dough into six equal sections. Gently roll each section into a 12-inch rope, then fold into a pretzel shape. 3. Place pretzels into ungreased air fryer basket. Adjust the temperature to 188°C and set the timer for 8 minutes, turning pretzels halfway through cooking. 4. In a small bowl, combine remaining butter, remaining sweetener, and cinnamon. Brush ½ mixture on both sides of pretzels. 5. Place pretzels back into air fryer and cook an additional 2 minutes at 188°C. 6. Transfer pretzels to a large plate. Brush on both sides with remaining butter mixture, then let cool 5 minutes before serving.

Fried Golden Bananas

Prep time: 5 minutes | Cook time: 7 minutes | Serves 6

1 large egg	3 bananas, halved crosswise
30 g cornflour	Cooking oil
30 g plain bread crumbs	Chocolate sauce, for drizzling

1. Preheat the air fryer to 192°C 2. Separate the biscuit dough into 8 biscuits and place them on a flat work surface. Use a small circle cookie cutter or a biscuit cutter to cut a hole in the center of each biscuit. You can also cut the holes using a knife. 3. Spray the air fryer basket with cooking oil. 4. Put 4 donuts in the air fryer. Do not stack. Spray with cooking oil. Air fry for 4 minutes. 5. Open the air fryer and flip the donuts. Air fry for an additional 4 minutes. 6. Remove the cooked donuts from the air fryer, then repeat steps 3 and 4 for the remaining 4 donuts. 7. Drizzle chocolate sauce over the donuts and enjoy while warm.

Tortilla Fried Pies

Prep time: 10 minutes | Cook time: 5 minutes per batch | Makes 12 pies

12 small flour tortillas (4-inch diameter)	2 tablespoons desiccated, unsweetened coconut
60 g fig jam	Oil for misting or cooking spray
30 g sliced almonds	

1. Wrap refrigerated tortillas in damp paper towels and heat in microwave 30 seconds to warm. 2. Working with one tortilla at a time, place 2 teaspoons fig jam, 1 teaspoon sliced almonds, and ½ teaspoon coconut in the center of each. 3. Moisten outer edges of tortilla all around. 4. Fold one side of tortilla over filling to make a half-moon shape and press down lightly on center. Using the tines of a fork, press down firmly on edges of tortilla to seal in filling. 5. Mist both sides with oil or cooking spray. 6. Place hand pies in air fryer basket close but not overlapping. It's fine to lean some against the sides and corners of the basket. You may need to cook in 2 batches. 7. Air fry at 200°C for 5 minutes or until lightly browned. Serve hot. 8. Refrigerate any leftover pies in a closed container. To serve later, toss them back in the air fryer basket and cook for 2 or 3 minutes to reheat.

Air Fryer Apple Fritters

Prep time: 30 minutes | Cook time: 7 to 8 minutes | Serves 6

125 g chopped, peeled Granny Smith apple	1 teaspoon salt
	2 tablespoons milk
60 g granulated sugar	2 tablespoons butter, melted
1 teaspoon ground cinnamon	1 large egg, beaten
125 g plain flour	Cooking spray
1 teaspoon baking powder	30 g icing sugar (optional)

1. Mix together the apple, granulated sugar, and cinnamon in a small bowl. Allow to sit for 30 minutes. 2. Combine the flour, baking powder, and salt in a medium bowl. Add the milk, butter, and egg and stir to incorporate. 3. Pour the apple mixture into the bowl of flour mixture and stir with a spatula until a dough forms. 4. Make the fritters: On a clean work surface, divide the dough into 12 equal portions and shape into 1-inch balls. Flatten them into patties with your hands. 5. Preheat the air fryer to 176°C. Line the air fryer basket with baking paper and spray it with cooking spray. 6. Transfer the apple fritters onto the baking paper, evenly spaced but not too close together. Spray the fritters with cooking spray. 7. Bake for 7 to 8 minutes until lightly browned. Flip the fritters halfway through the cooking time. 8. Remove from the basket to a plate and serve with the icing sugar sifted on top, if desired.

Printed in Great Britain
by Amazon

87260120R00038